MW01702691

Business Fundamentals
from
Harvard Business School Publishing

# UNDERSTANDING CONSUMER BEHAVIOR

HBS Publishing

## CONTENTS

# INTRODUCTION

Welcome to the Business Fundamentals series from Harvard Business School Publishing.

Most of the readings in this collection were developed for the MBA or executive education programs of Harvard Business School. These programs rely heavily on the case method of instruction, in which students analyze and discuss firsthand accounts of actual management situations. Students also learn the fundamentals of what managers do: how they gather information, make choices, organize their activities, and measure performance. At Harvard Business School, the fundamentals are often taught through background notes -- such as those in this collection -- that describe business processes, management techniques, and industries.

The collections in this series are not meant to be comprehensive, but to present the fundamentals of business. This collection contains five notes, plus a consumer research exercise, and one article each from *Harvard Business Review* and *California Management Review* (*CMR* articles are available from HBS Publishing). Collectively, these materials provide a framework for assessing, interpreting, and (when possible!) managing consumer behavior. The readings concentrate mainly on consumer goods and markets, but several have clear applications to industrial customers as well.

Because the readers emphasize currency, our usual objective is to include items published within the past five years. Nearly all the items herein were published since 1999 -- but we gladly broke our rule to make room for the opening consumer behavior exercise, written in 1995 by HBS professors Susan Fournier and John Deighton.

The Business Fundamentals collections are designed for both individual study and facilitated training. For each reading we have provided a summary, outline, learning objectives, and a group of questions, ideas, and exercises. If these readings are part of a training program in your company, you will find them to be a rich resource for discussion and group work.

You can search for related materials -- or order extra copies of a particular reading -- on our Web site: www.hbsp.harvard.edu.

Thank you for choosing this Business Fundamentals title. We are confident that your learning experience will be rewarding.

The Editors

## CONSUMER BEHAVIOR EXERCISES

(S. Fournier and J. Deighton / #9-596-039 and 9-596-042 / 2p each)

### Special Note About the Consumer Behavior Exercises

This pair of items represents a group of six exercises identified as Consumer Behavior Exercises A through F. Typically, the exercises are assigned to six teams within an MBA class; each team administers an exercise to a number of consumers, then discusses or writes about its findings and also learns about the findings of the other five groups.

*Odds are that you are not planning to divide a group of your colleagues into six teams and conduct the exercises in typical fashion -- but that doesn't mean that you should miss out on the intellectual value of the exercises. To help you realize that value, we've given you all the basic materials without excess paper.* Here's the key:

The exercises differ from one another in two key respects:

1. A, B, and C all contain the same set of questions designed to audit the consumer choice process, while D, E, and F all contain a different set of questions designed to audit usage, or the relationship between the consumer and the product or service.
2. Both sets of questions are to be applied to purchases of differing expense or purpose:
   - A and D to "a mundane product or service costing $5 or less"
   - B and E to "a product or service costing over $100 that performs a utilitarian function"
   - C and F to "a product or service costing over $100 that, the customer feels, reveals something about the kind of person he or she is."

To make matters simple, we've included here exercises A and D, which contain the different sets of questions for the consumer. Try all six variants of the exercise with at least a few friends, colleagues, or acquaintances. Or you might pick the product type that corresponds best to your work situation and ask a group of customers about it, using the questions from exercise A for half of the group and those from exercise D for the other half.

### Learning Objectives

- Cultivate empathy for the lived experience of the consumer.
- Encourage appreciation of the complexity of consumer behavior phenomena.
- Experience some issues and problems involved in conducting qualitative interviews and analyzing the information collected.
- Build a vocabulary for discussing consumer behavior issues.

### Questions, Ideas, and Exercises

1. How did the responses of customers to the "choice" questions from exercise A match up with those of customers who answered the "usage" questions from exercise D?

(You might consider making a list of all the factors that might have created these differences.) What do the differing responses suggest about such issues as brand loyalty (e.g., the likelihood that your customers are likely to be repeat buyers)?

2. Try all three product categories noted above. If your company doesn't make products in all three categories, use other products as examples -- the objective is to learn more about how consumers behave and how they understand and explain their own behaviors. Note especially the difference between the second and third product categories: the price guideline is the same, but one involves a utilitarian use and the other self-expression.

# Consumer Behavior Exercise (A)

The purpose of this exercise is to broaden your understanding of consumer behavior by bringing you face-to-face with a customer. The first step is to find a person who is not a member of this course, and who has recently bought a product or service of the kind defined in the box below. This customer could be an institutional/industrial buyer if you prefer.

Your assignment is to conduct a depth interview of about 30-60 minutes in length with this customer. The goal of the interview is to understand the decision process that governed the purchase of this product or service in terms that can be useful to a marketing manager.

The list of questions on the back of this sheet is intended as a broad guide around which you can structure your depth interview. It is not to be followed dogmatically. Nor is it complete and exhaustive of the types of questions you need to ask, or the level of detail for which you need to probe. Rather you should try to stimulate a lively and open discussion around these key question areas from which you can: (a) develop a deep understanding of the purchase decision process; and (b) surface the factors, in the environment and in the customer's psyche, that really determined why the customer acted the way s/he did.

Be prepared to report briefly and concisely to the class on your key insights. You will probably find it useful to summarize your thoughts in writing (1-2 pages).

**A. A mundane product or service costing less than $5.**

*This exercise was prepared by Professors John Deighton and Susan Fournier.*

## General Discussion Areas

### Your task is to audit the choice process.

#### Who was the decision making unit?

- Who bought the product or service?
- Identify all those who played a role in the decision process. What role did they play?

#### What motivated the purchase?

- What problems did the product/service solve? What functions would it facilitate?
- What attributes seemed important?

#### Characterize the decision.

- Was it a first-time decision? A review of a previous decision? A careful decision? A casual decision? Was the amount of deliberation appropriate to the decision?

#### Characterize the decision-making process.

- What triggered the process?
- Was there an information search? How was the search conducted? How much information was collected? What sources were used? When in the process was information gathered?
- How many alternatives were evaluated? Why those?
- How was the final choice determined?

#### Where did the consumer buy?

- Why there?
- Which came first: where to buy or what to buy?

# Consumer Behavior Exercise (D)

The purpose of this exercise is to broaden your understanding of consumer behavior by bringing you face-to-face with a customer. The first step is to find a person who is not a member of this course, and who is using a product or service of the kind defined in the box below. This customer could be an institutional/industrial user if you prefer.

Your assignment is to conduct a depth interview of about 30-60 minutes in length with this customer. The goal of the interview is to understand how the owner or user feels about the product or service in terms that can be useful to a marketing manager.

The list of questions on the back of this sheet is intended as a broad guide around which you can structure your depth interview. It is not to be followed dogmatically. Nor is it complete and exhaustive of the types of questions you need to ask, or the level of detail for which you need to probe. Rather you should try to stimulate a lively and open discussion around these key question areas from which you can: (a) develop a deep understanding of the ownership/usage experience; and (b) surface the factors, in the environment and in the customer's psyche, that determine why the customer acts, thinks, and feels the way s/he does.

Be prepared to report briefly and concisely to the class on your key insights. You will probably find it useful to summarize your thoughts in writing (1-2 pages).

**D. A mundane product or service costing less than $5.**

*This exercise was prepared by Professors John Deighton and Susan Fournier.*

## General Discussion Areas

**Your task is to audit the relationship between the consumer and the product/service.**

### How would you describe the consumption experience?

- How is the product/service used or consumed? Who uses it? When? Where? How often? What feelings and opinions surround the consumption experience?

### What type of a relationship does the customer have with the product or service?

- How long has the relationship been going on? How has it evolved and changed over time? What terms best describe the relationship: good, bad, mixed, love-hate, dependency, casual, partners, exploited, exploitative, good friends?

### What kinds of things have gone wrong in the relationship?

- Stockouts, unavailability of parts of service, inappropriate communication, quality lapses, violations of norms or expectations or values.

### What positive surprises have occurred?

- Exceptional service, welcome communication, performance above expectations, affirmation of values.

### Is the customer satisfied or dissatisfied with the product or service?

- What factors influence the level of felt (dis)satisfaction? How were expectations formed? Did the product exceed them or fall short? How?

### What is the meaning of this product or service to the customer?

- How does the product fit into the consumer's life? What role does it play?

### What role does the brand play in all of this?

## ANALYZING CONSUMER PERCEPTIONS

(R. Dolan / #9-599-110 / 13 p)

### Summary

Explains perceptual mapping techniques in a non-technical fashion. The procedure is useful for the depiction of the structure of the market. Discusses alternative methods, presents examples of each, and shows how the maps can be used in marketing decision making.

### Outline

Introduction
Section I: Data Collection and Profile Analysis
Section II: Perceptual Mapping Techniques
Section III: Applying the Maps in New Product Development

### Learning Objectives

- Learn techniques of capturing consumers' view of a firm, brand, or product relative to competitors.
- Deepen skills at analyzing information collected from consumers.

### Questions, Ideas, and Exercises

1. If your company has done consumer perception research, try illustrating the results through perceptual mapping techniques, then gather colleagues together to determine what the maps show about the structure of your market. Make sure you choose mapping techniques that reveal clearly whether your intended product positioning has been achieved and how your competitors are viewed. Are there any "holes" in the product space that might represent product niches overlooked by all suppliers?

2. How would your firm ideally design a study of consumer perceptions of a new product concept? What attributes are most important in your market? Which customers would you call on, and by what means would you identify prospective customers? Given the nature of your products, would a concept statement suffice or would the test consumers need to see or use a prototype?

9-599-110
REV: DECEMBER 12, 2001

ROBERT J. DOLAN

# Analyzing Consumer Perceptions

## *Introduction*

An important input to marketing decision making is often an understanding of how consumers "see" the firm, brand, or product relative to competitors. In setting an objective of a particular "product positioning" in the mind of the consumer, we want to check whether or not the desired positioning has in fact been achieved. This helps us assess whether the current strategy is on target, or if some "repositioning" is necessary.

For example, in "Black and Decker: Power Tools" case,[1] management commissioned surveys to

- Obtain tradesmen perceptions of the "overall quality" of 11 brands of tools
- Compare perceptions of the Black and Decker brand vs. those of key competitors Makita and Milwaukee on six dimensions:
    - Is "one of best"
    - High-quality tool
    - Durable tool
    - Proud to own
    - Stands behind product
    - Easy-to-get service

These perceptual data were critical in diagnosing Black and Decker's problem and suggesting the most beneficial type of strategy change.

Similarly, in "L'Oréal of Paris: Bringing 'Class to Mass' with Plenitude,"[2] management collected data to understand consumers' perceptions of Plenitude and of key competitors' products, including Ponds, Oil of Olay, and Estee Lauder, on 15 dimensions, such as "technologically advanced," "good value for the money," "relieves dryness" and "available in stores where you shop." In the L'Oréal case, the consumer perception data were statistically analyzed to produce a two-dimensional visual representation of the competing brands' position on the attributes.

[1] "The Black and Decker Corporation (A): Power Tools Division," HBS No. 595-057.

[2] HBS No. 598-056.

Professor Robert J. Dolan prepared this note as the basis for class discussion.

Section I of this note first describes the collection of perception data and the reporting of those data in a "profile analysis." This is a very simple procedure, often quite appropriate to the problem at hand.

Section II discusses the more advanced procedure of creating a "perceptual map" as done by L'Oreal. There are two types of data from which these maps can be created. We provide some intuition for how each works and present the advantages and disadvantages of each.

Section III discusses sample applications and uses in marketing decision making. While we do not discuss the details of the statistical procedures, we provide insight into what is happening in the data analysis phase.

## *Section I: Data Collection and Profile Analysis*

There is a variety of ways in which to collect perception data. L'Oréal used a 1-10 scale and asked respondents to provide a rating to indicate the extent to which they agreed with statements of the following sort:

Plenitude is "technologically advanced"

Where 1 = completely disagree

10 = completely agree

Henkel, a Germany-based competitor of L'Oréal mentioned in the case, in addition to selling skin care products has a diverse set of other products, including adhesives. It used the same approach in assessing the image of its adhesive brands, Pritt and Pattex.[3]

A commonly used variant of the rating scale is the semantic differential scale having five or seven points with polar adjectives at either end of the spectrum. For example, to assess its position vs. Sony, Barco management could commission a survey in which respondents are asked to give their perceptions of the brand by marking the following:

Barco Projectors are:

| | | | | | | |
|---|---|---|---|---|---|---|
| Unreliable | ______ | ______ | ______ | ______ | ______ | Reliable |
| Hard-to-Use | ______ | ______ | ______ | ______ | ______ | Easy-to-Use |
| Low Priced | ______ | ______ | ______ | ______ | ______ | High Priced |
| Poor Value | ______ | ______ | ______ | ______ | ______ | Good Value |
| Fuzzy Output | ______ | ______ | ______ | ______ | ______ | Sharp Output |

When analyzing *perception* data (what people see) as opposed to *preference* data (what people like), we usually are more willing to live with an assumption of homogeneity in responses across consumers. For example, you and I are both likely to perceive Volvo as a "safe" car. But, it is dangerous to assume that you and I are similar in our desire for a safe car.

[3] "Henkel Group: Umbrella Branding and Globalization Decisions," HBS No. 585-185.

We can check on how similar are perceptions across respondents (e.g., just compute the variance of the ratings on an attribute across consumers). If one suspects that perceptions vary across groups (e.g., West Coast vs. East Coast, Inexperienced Users vs. Experienced Users, Young vs. Old), you can break out the data and look at specific groups. If we are willing to assume perceptions are pretty much the same across respondents, we can then easily summarize the data by averaging it across all survey respondents. Henkel in analyzing its Pritt adhesive brand had 100 respondents and found an average rating of 6.8 (on the 1-10 "strongly disagree" to "strongly agree" scale) for the statement "Pritt Conveys Confidence." After averaging across respondents, a useful visual representation is Profile Analysis, known more commonly and colloquially as a "snake plot." This simply plots the ratings of brands by attribute. Henkel developed this comparison for its light-duty Pritt brand vs. leading competitor Uhu on 18 attributes using the same 1-10 scale. The raw data were:

| | Score on 1-10 Scale<br>1 = Completely Disagree<br>10 = Completely Agree | |
|---|---|---|
| | **Pritt** | **Uhu** |
| Conveys confidence | 6.8 | 8.5 |
| Is of high quality | 7.2 | 8.4 |
| Is for special uses only | 6.5 | 5.5 |
| Is only for sticking paper | 5.7 | 4.3 |
| Is somehow likeable | 6.4 | 7.2 |
| Glues reliably | 7.1 | 8.4 |
| Is of great strength | 6.9 | 8,3 |
| Is a well-known brand | 7.9 | 9.7 |
| Is for general purposes | 6.5 | 8.1 |
| Is usually reasonably priced | 6.5 | 6.7 |
| Is sold everywhere | 7.4 | 8.9 |
| Offers all adhesives you need | 7.1 | 8.3 |
| Is more for children | 4.9 | 4.5 |
| Is more known from the office | 6.3 | 5.6 |
| Offers useful adhesives | 8.0 | 8.7 |
| Has a well-structured range | 6.9 | 7.9 |
| Is something for experts | 2.4 | 3.0 |
| Is clean in use | 7.6 | 7.7 |

(Numbers in table represent average rating score across 100 respondents.)

The corresponding Profile Analysis looks like this:

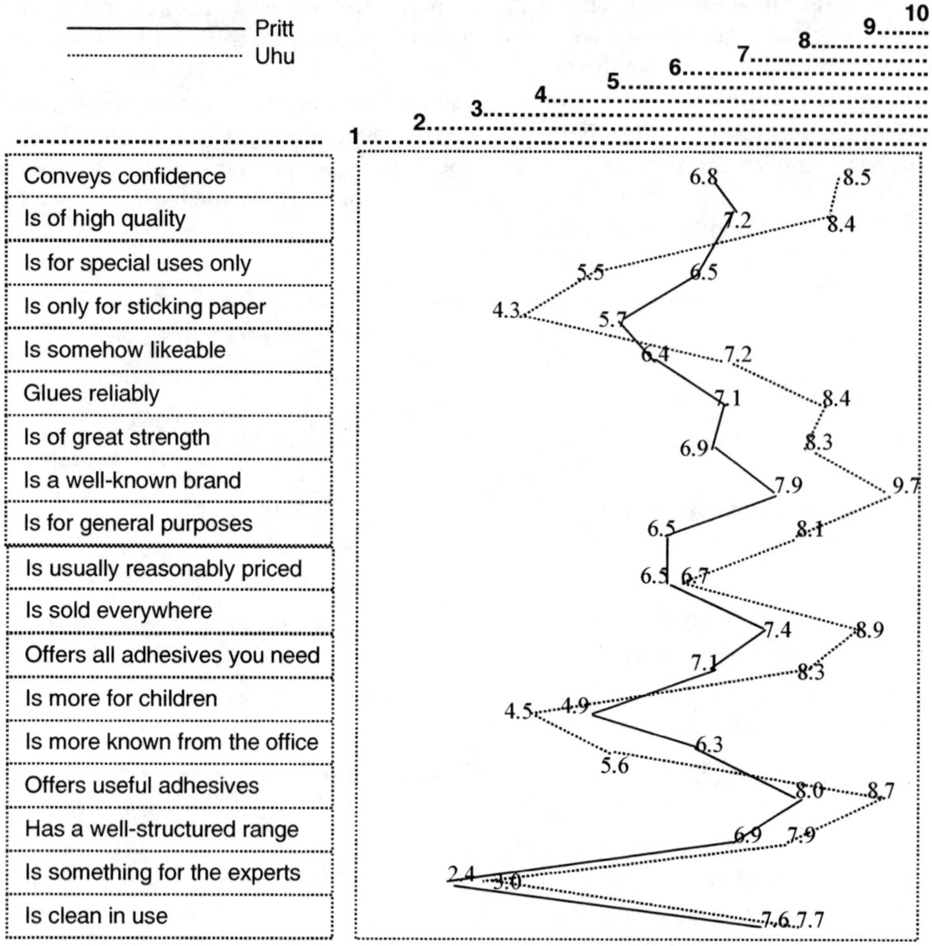


The plot pretty quickly gives insight into Pritt's relative position—Uhu being seen as the stronger, general-purpose brand and Pritt's strength being confined to special light-duty purpose like sticking paper for children.

The utility of "snake plots" depends a lot on how many brands have to be considered in the analysis. Given the market situation, Henkel appropriately considered just Uhu. So, the "snake plot" was a powerful enough approach. However, as the number of brands to be considered increases (as it did for L'Oreal with eight brands to consider), snake plots can become an uninterpretable mess, and more powerful techniques are typically needed to yield the desired insights. This is why perceptual mapping techniques have been developed and are widely used.

## *Section II: Perceptual Mapping Techniques*

When consumers' perceptions of multiple competitors on multiple dimensions are of interest, more powerful analysis techniques help to make the data more meaningful. Perceptual mapping techniques derive their name from the fact that the output is a map of brands depicted in attribute space. There are two types of mapping procedures, depending on the type of data collected from consumers: (i) ratings of items on prespecified attributes and (ii) judgments on overall similarity of pairs of brands. The second method is particularly useful when articulating the attributes of interest in a category is difficult. For example, it may be difficult to state in a meaningful way the attributes consumers use to differentiate types of fruit, perfumes, and styles of office chairs. We now discuss each method in turn.

**Attribute Rating Method** As mentioned above, L'Oreal used the attribute rating method for eight brands on 15 attributes. In an industrial content, Dow's Specialty Chemical Group[4] used this approach to assess consumers' perception of Dow vs. Competitors on 8 attributes:

1. Meets scheduled delivery dates
2. Practices innovation and development
3. Has fair pricing
4. Has consistent products
5. Provides support in solving processing problems
6. Has custom color capability
7. Provides adequate technical literature
8. Withstands high heat distortion temperatures

The value of perceptual mapping is that it gives us a pictorial representation to summarize the data. The Dow situation had a small "data matrix," consisting of 32 cell entries.

| | 1 | 2 | 3 | 4 | 5 | 6 | 7 | 8 |
|---|---|---|---|---|---|---|---|---|
| DOW | | | | | | | | |
| **Competitor #1** | | | | | | | | |
| **Competitor #2** | | | | | | | | |
| **Competitor #3** | | | | | | | | |

**Rating on Attribute #**

A cell entry in the data matrix is the average rating of the competitor represented by the row on the attribute represented by the column. Even the relatively small data matrix of Dow would be hard to summarize without recourse to statistical procedures.

The statistical procedure underlying this type of perceptual mapping is typically either factor analysis or discriminant analysis. Intuitively, what the procedures do is "look" at situations such as shown in **Figure A**. In panel #1 of **Figure A**, imagine that we have to plot four vendors on two attributes. We see all vendors are rated identically for attribute #1—Meets Delivery Dates—so that is not a very interesting product feature in terms of differentiating products from one another. Once the statistical analysis reveals this, it does not give the attribute "Delivery Dates" much importance in

[4] R.H. Siemer, "Using Perceptual Mapping for Market Entry Decisions," 1989 Sawtooth Software Conference Proceedings, pp. 107-114.

portraying the situation. Attribute #2—"Innovation"—on the other hand, varies across products and would have a place in the final map. Panel #2 of **Figure A** is a situation in which attributes #5 "Provides Support" and #7 "Provides Adequate Technical Literature" are mapped. The result shown here is that these attributes are highly correlated (i.e., the vendors rated high on #5 are also rated high on #7). The statistical analysis would thus treat attributes #5 and #7 as measurements of the same underlying construct.

**Figure A** Intuition Behind Perceptual Mapping

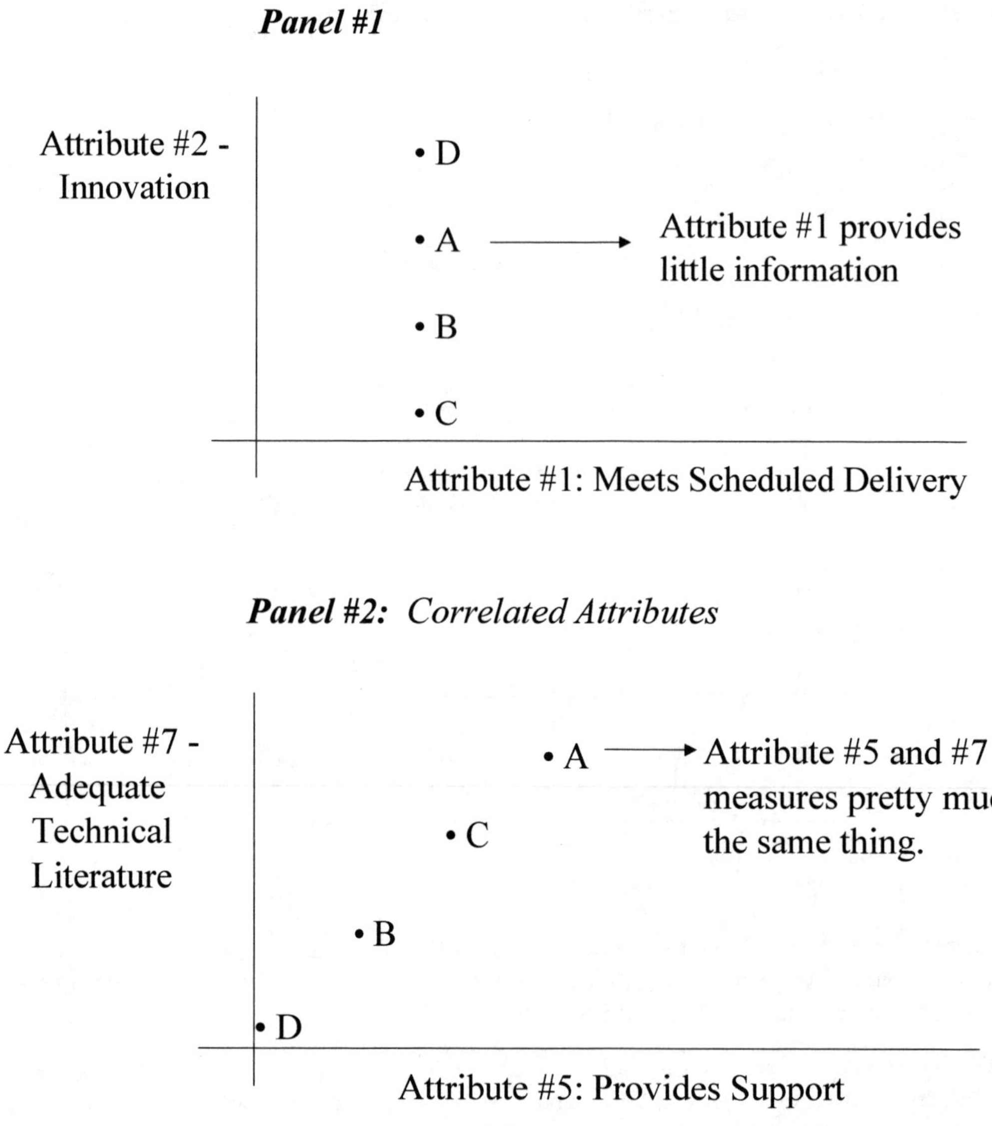


The analysis for Dow collapses the original set of 8 attributes to a two-dimensional map with the four vendors positioned on the axes. Since the original data are in eight dimensions (attributes) and the perceptual map is reduced down to two, the map cannot capture all the variation among the vendors given in the data matrix. However, essentially it does the best it can (i.e., retains the most important information from the full data matrix and reports it in two dimensions to provide visual impact).

The precise output or form of the map depends on the particular mapping software used. Generally, multiple attributes are shown in a two-dimensional space by varying the angle with which the vector comes out of the origin. For example, the L'Oreal map (case **Exhibit 9**) is reproduced here in **Figure B**.

**Figure B** L'Oreal Map

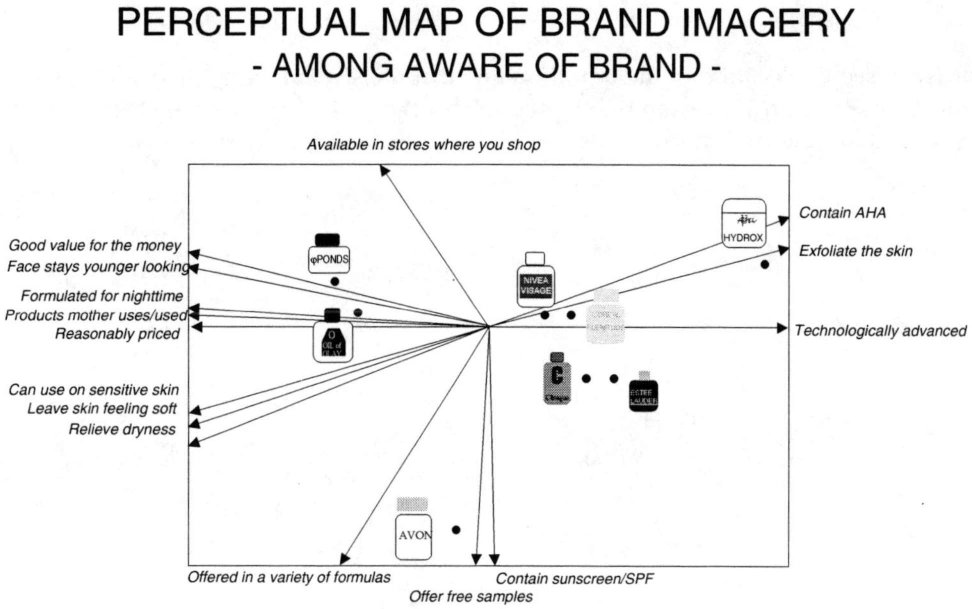


Let's pull out four of the vectors and focus on interpreting them.

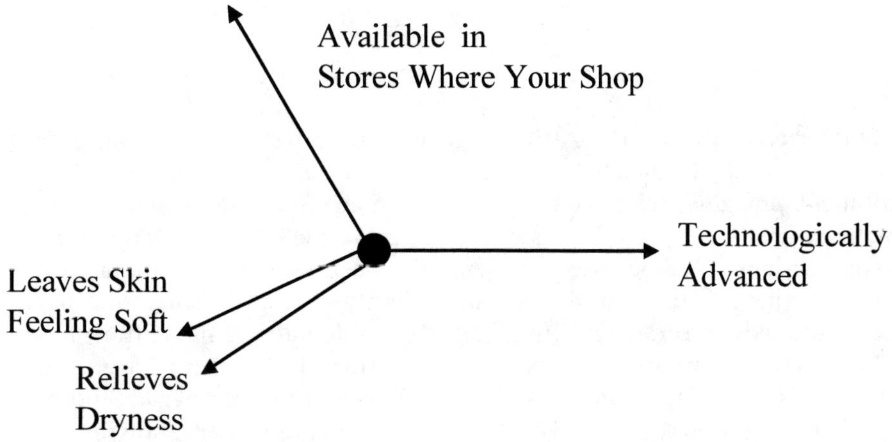


We see two of the vectors go in the same general direction. What this shows us is that brands which rated "high" on "relieves dryness" were also rated "high" on "leaves skin feeling soft." In other words, there really is only one underlying idea here—it's like attributes 5 and 7 in **Figure A—** Panel #2. In contrast, "Available in Stores Where You Shop" forms an almost 90° angle with the softness/dryness vectors, indicating it is unrelated to the softness/dryness skin dimension (i.e., a brand's position on softness/dry skin does not tell you much about its position on "available"). The

"Technologically Advanced" vector points almost in the other direction from softness/dry—capturing the fact that the brands on the market are currently perceived as trading off technologically advanced vs. softness/dryness (i.e., if you are "high" on one you are "low" on the other).

In L'Oreal's case shown in **Figure B**, all vectors were shown with the same length. However, sometimes the vector length is also varied across attributes to indicate how well the provided map is capturing the actual variance in scores across brands for that attribute. The software in Lilien and Rangaswamy's *New Product and Brand Management: Marketing Engineering Applications*[5] Positioning Analysis (p. 50) uses this convention.

In order to see the location of the brand on an attribute, you always "drop a perpendicular" from the brand to the vector. For example, to see where the eight brands in L'Oreal are positioned on dryness, we extend the "relieves dryness" vector back through the origin (shown by the dotted line)

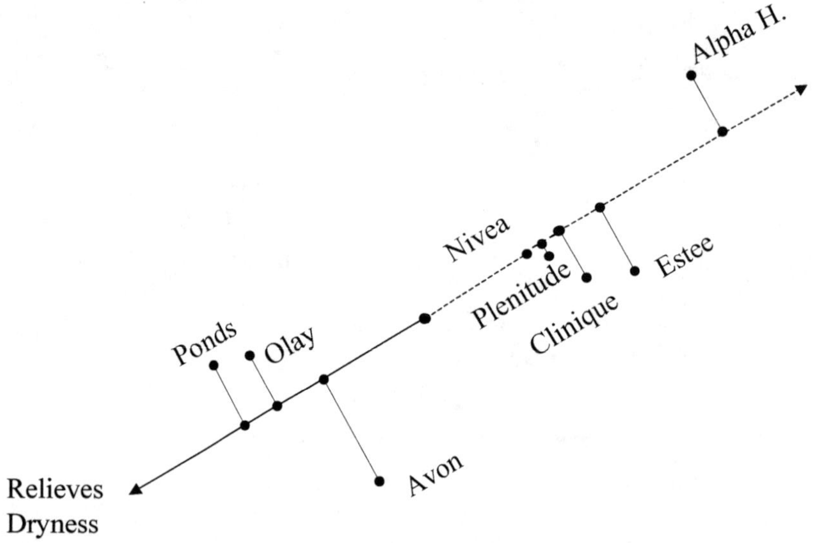


and move along a line to the vector, such that the line forms a 90° angle with the vector.

**Overall Similarity Method** The Attribute Rate Method has a key limitation for some product types (i.e., it requires the researcher to articulate and the respondent to think in terms of specific product attributes). Imagine trying to execute the approach in the soft drink or perfume market. In categories with competition driven by tastes, odors, or aesthetics—(i.e., things we do not verbalize very well)—the attribute method breaks down. For such situations, an alternative is to ask the respondent to make judgments about the overall similarity of pairs of items. Specifically, for *n* items, we require the respondent to rank the [(n)(n-1)]÷2 possible pairs of items from *most similar* to *least similar*. For example, mapping the theme park attractions in Southern Florida market we might consider 6 items: Disney's Magic Kingdom, Disney's Epcot Center, Universal Studios, MGM Studios, Sea World, and Busch Gardens. (Note: we limit this to 6 for simplicity in showing how the procedure works. Ordinarily, one would want to consider all relevant competition.) With 6 items, there are 15 pairs. A convenient way to represent the required input is in matrix form with a 1 = most similar pair and a 15 = least similar pair. Suppose one respondent gave the judgments shown in **Table A**:

[5] G. Lilien and A. Rangaswamy, *New Product and Brand Management: Marketing Engineering Applications* (Reading, Mass: Addison Wesley, 1999)

**Table A** Respondent Ranking of Similarity of Six Theme Park Attractions

| | Universal | MGM | Sea World | Magic Kingdom | Epcot |
|---|---|---|---|---|---|
| Busch Gardens | 11 | 12 | 10 | 6 | 13 |
| Universal | -- | 1 | 14 | 2 | 5 |
| MGM | | -- | 15 | 3 | 6 |
| Sea World | | | -- | 8 | 9 |
| Magic Kingdom | | | | -- | 4 |
| Epcot | | | | | -- |

"Eyeballing" the data, we might notice a couple of things. First, Magic Kingdom is seen as pretty similar to all the others—it is pretty mainstream. Also, the Sea World-Epcot pair is rated ninth—less similar than the average pair. This might seem odd as they are two of the more educational offerings in the set. In order to sort these things out, we submit the data to a statistical procedure, to develop a map to permit us to "see" the data and get the information from it.

The statistical procedure is called multidimensional scaling, often referred to as MDS. It attempts to find a map such that the distance between the attractions as shown on the map match up (i.e., be in the same order) as the rank numbers in the input data matrix of **Table A**. The map in **Figure C** fits this bill. The output of multidimensional scaling is a plot like **Figure C** and a statistic which tells how closely the distances on the map match up with the original input data. Note that we do not know what the axes are—but our knowledge of the category can help us to name them. On the vertical axis, it's Busch Gardens, MGM Studios, and Universal Studios on one end vs. Epcot and Sea World on the other. This suggests a thrill ride/entertainment vs. educational dimension. The horizontal axis may represent value for the money as two attractions with frequent price promotions (Busch Gardens and Sea World) are set against those with perceived higher prices. The map helps explain what might seem odd to us from "eyeballing" the data. While Sea World and Epcot are seen as similar in their educational aspect, this respondent differentiates them on the basis of their value/price.

**Figure C** Perceptual Map of Theme Park Attractions

The overall similarity method thus allows us not only to map products but also infer the attributes used by the respondent in making distinctions. Note, however, that these inferences were somewhat subjective (e.g., one might say the horizontal axis is expected wait time at attractions).

Examples of use are in mapping retail stores, desserts, food products, and ethical drugs. Kotler[6] reports actual application to California amusement attractions using overall similarities.

**Table B** summarizes the major differences between methods.

**Table B** Comparison of Methods

| Attribute Rating | Overall Similarity |
|---|---|
| Input Data | |
| • brand ratings on attributes | • overall similarity ranking |
| • attributes prespecified by analyst | • definition of similarity left to respondent |
| Statistical Technique | |
| • factor analysis<br>or<br>multiple discriminant analysis<br>(software generally available) | • multidimensional scaling (special-purpose software required; however, efficient packages available at low cost) |
| Output | |
| • product positions on axes | • relative product positions; axes must be interpreted by analyst |
| Best Suited For | |
| • applications with "hard" attributes which can be verbalized | • categories dominated by not easily articulated attributes |

## *Section III: Applying the Maps in New Product Development*

There are three major ways in which perceptual maps are used in marketing:

i. to obtain a better understanding of current positioning and market structure
ii. to test where a new product being considered for introduction would be perceived
iii. to provide direction to R&D efforts to satisfy the wants of consumers better.

In many studies, perceptual maps are used for all three of these purposes simultaneously. The third is somewhat different from the others in that it requires representation of consumers' preferred positions (we usually refer to this as "ideal points") as well as competitors' positions on the map. We will now cover each of the three purposes in turn.

**Purpose #1: Understanding Market Structure** As noted at the outset, one often would like to check rigorously that the desired product positioning has been attained. Understanding where we

[6] P. Kotler, *Marketing Management*, 9th ed. (N.J.: Prentice-Hall, Inc., 1997).

are seen relative to the competition facilitates this. Also, at the idea-generation stage of the new product development process, perceptual maps can be a useful stimulus to opportunity identification. "Holes" in the product space might be exploited as they may represent niches of the market which current competitors have overlooked and could be developed. Second, the maps indicate the vulnerability of competitors by showing how consumers perceive them. For example, there are cases where a dominant share brand seems impossible to attack. However, a deeper understanding of customers' attitudes and perceptions can show the means of attacking this seemingly impregnable incumbent.

**Purpose #2: Perceptions of a Product Concept** Once a general opportunity has been identified (either with or without perceptual maps), the process usually moves forward to concept development and testing. Perceptual maps can be used to test if the concept or product would be perceived by consumers as the firm intended.

For this use, respondents must be informed about the new concept or product, either through a concept statement or, if possible, product use. Once they are able to form their own image and judgments about the brand, the method proceeds as usual.

For example, suppose a firm in the computer business already participates in the market and the key attributes are ease of use, flexibility, and price. A Perceptual Map of the market on flexibility and ease of use is shown in **Figure D.**

**Figure D** Perceptual Map of Personal Computer Market

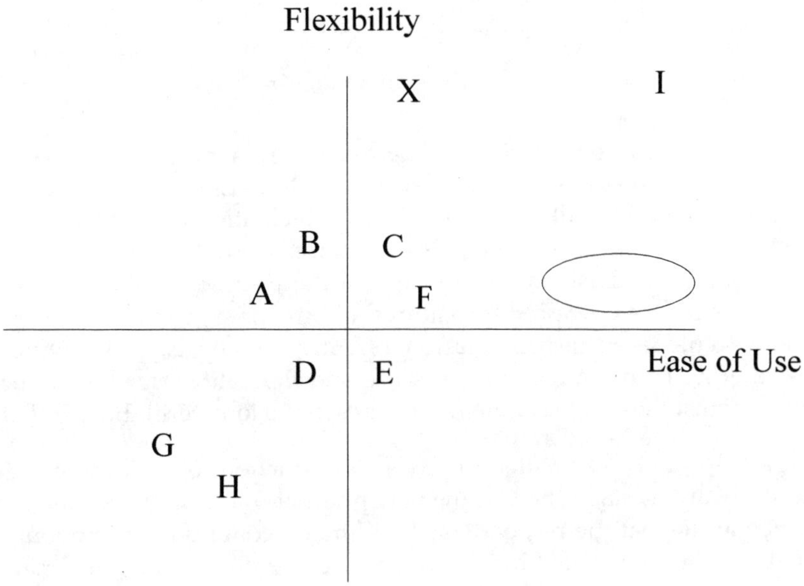


The map shows a group of competitors in the middle of the map; firms G and H in the southwest corner offer less flexibility and convenience (presumably at lower prices). Our Firm X has been able to differentiate itself from the group via innovation on flexibility, taking point X on the map. Although not depicted on the map, this is at a slight price premium over the offerings of A, B, C, D, E, and F. Firm I has been able to differentiate itself by offering both greater flexibility and greater ease of use, but its offering is at a significant price premium.

Our firm is considering expanding its product line to bring out a machine which is very easy to use, but with average flexibility (i.e., a product to be located in the area of the circle drawn on the map). Such a product would sell at the same price level as X, but would (it was hoped) not cannibalize X but rather appeal to a market segment now buying F or I. The question is whether the product could take on this position in customers' eyes even if, in a technical performance sense, it provided average flexibility but was quite easy to use. Perceptual mapping can provide an answer to the advisability of the strategy. Once consumers understand the proposed product, a mapping study could be done to see where the new product falls. **Figure E** shows the four zones.

**Figure E**

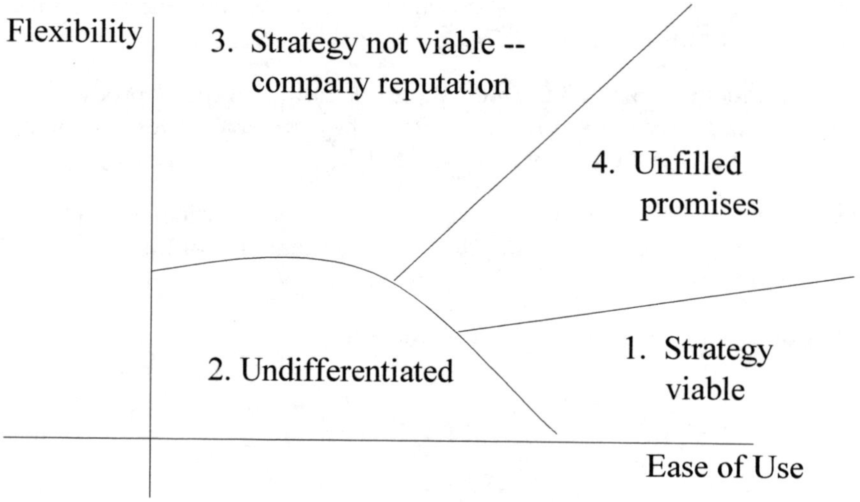


If the new product takes on a position in consumers' eyes in Zone 1, the basic positioning is viable. The product is positioned strongly on the ease-of-use dimension, and the tradeoff of ease of use with flexibility is communicated. All other zones are problematic. Zone 2 puts the firm "in the bunch" with firms A, B, C, D, E, and F—not differentiated enough to make a product line extension worthwhile. Zone 3 is a basic failure to capture the desired position. The firm's reputation for flexibility overwhelms the new product features and the new product is seen to have the same basic strengths and weaknesses as the firm's current offering. Finally, Zone 4 may initially look like a good place to be—offering both improved ease-of-use and flexibility over the "bunch"—but the product cannot deliver against those expectations and hence in the long term this would be problematic.

Similarly, a map can be used after a product introduction to track the positioning. For example, suppose the study at this stage showed the new product to be on the border between Zones 1 and 4. One might then argue that the respondents had limited communication about the new product and that an actual introduction would be accompanied by extensive company-managed communication and trade press reviews which would be sufficient to place the product squarely in Zone 1—the "strategy viable" zone. Perceptual maps could be constructed after the introduction to test this hypothesis and aid in the determination of whether remedial action was necessary.

**Purpose #3: Direction to R&D Efforts to Satisfy Customers Better** This purpose is similar to Purpose #2, except here we require formal representation of the "ideal point" of a customer (i.e., what point on the map represents the ideal combination of attributes for different customer groups). Our example in Purpose #2 was chosen to sidestep this issue by choosing two attributes which almost everybody would like as much of as could be obtained for a given price. Consequently, we could think of the "ideal" being as far to the northeast as possible.

When we have attributes for which more is not necessarily better, we will want to represent explicitly these ideals. There are two methods for doing this, both of which are applicable in either the attribute rating or overall similarity procedure. For the attribute approach, we alter the input data collection phase to include the respondents' "ideal" in the set of things to be rated on each attribute. In the overall similarity approach, we include the "ideal" as one of the objects in forming all possible pairs for similarity ranking.

The examples in the literature point out the value of doing this because the ideal points of individuals, while usually clustered, are spread out across the map of brands. For example, Johnson's[7] work on presidential candidates identified eight clusters with significantly varied ideals on the two key dimensions of candidate differentiation:

- liberal versus conservative
- reduce government involvement versus increase government involvement.

Often the intent is to use perceptual maps to serve each of these three purposes. The potential for managerial utility is hopefully clear from the description of the technique; however, added testimony comes from the number of firms regularly using the method and the reaction of some of those users. For example, in discussing Dow Chemical's application in the specialty plastics market, Siemer[8] notes the following contributions of the perceptual mapping study:

> Some of the facts we learned from this study shocked us.... We had focused on physical product benefits as a basis for competitive advantage. Instead, we found a market more interested in service issues. [The study provided] greater understanding of the market structure ... an understanding of the unique needs of industry segments [and] ... competitors' vulnerabilities from the point of view of our customers.

The impact of this improved understanding was a change in Dow's basic approach to the market and spending plans, that is to say, "we were able to develop a strategic positioning for Dow that focused and prioritized our resources where they would have the greatest competitive advantage, and then were able to abandon issues and priorities that had low potential return because of customer indifference."

* * * * *

Perceptual mapping has proven an extremely useful addition to the marketing analysis toolkit. It does have a number of limitations, however, which should be noted. First, it presents a static view (i.e., it is a snapshot of consumers' current perceptions). If a series of studies of the same market is done over time, some trends can be monitored. Second, while it may help a firm determine what it would like to do vis-à-vis the market, it provides no indication of the cost or likelihood of being able to achieve the desired positioning.

In short, it in no way substitutes for management judgment but often provides valuable input and serves as a very useful focal point in strategic planning discussions.

---

[7] R.M. Johnson, "Adaptive Perceptual Mapping," Sawtooth Software Conference on Perceptual Mapping, Conjoint Analysis, and Computer Interviewing, 1987, pp. 143-158.

[8] R.H. Siemer, "Using Perceptual Mapping for Market-Entry Decisions," 1989 Sawtooth Software Conference Proceedings, pp. 107-114.

## ANALYZING CONSUMER PREFERENCES

(R. Dolan / #9-599-112 / 14 p)

### Summary

Presents a non-traditional description of the conjoint analysis methodology. Discusses the process by which a study is done and cites areas of application.

### Outline

Introduction
Section I: Concept Testing
Section II: Conjoint Analysis
General Conjoint Decision Issues

### Learning Objectives

- Learn basic elements of concept testing, including executing a concept test, working with various data types, and interpreting purchase intent data.
- Learn a multistep program for conducting conjoint analysis.
- Explore concepts and issues behind the successful practice of conjoint analysis.

### Questions, Ideas, and Exercises

1. The author provides a detailed example of conjoint-analysis research conducted for a new automobile code-named LION. Try developing a comparable test design for one of your company's new-product or product-revision ideas. See if you can carry it through to the market simulation stage. Share your design with a few colleagues and, if appropriate, propose using it in an actual customer test.

2. In the LION research noted above, the researchers found a surprising response to the question about environmental performance. In previous automobile research, customers had weighted that aspect heavily *in the abstract*; in this research, however, customers had to give up power or price in order to get environmental performance, and they were disinclined to do so. Consider the possible application of this outcome to your own customers: Are you assuming they value absolutely what they might really value only in the abstract?

9-599-112
REV: DECEMBER 12, 2001

ROBERT J. DOLAN

# Analyzing Consumer Preferences

## *Introduction*

Consumer preferences are at the heart of marketing. When we analyze consumer behavior, we are typically assessing how consumers make purchase decisions (i.e., the process via which they come to value one purchase alternative over another). Understanding of consumer preferences is particularly important for product policy (e.g., what features to have, whether or not to offer a new product) and pricing decisions.

Two procedures with proven utility for the actionable analysis of consumer preferences are

1. Concept testing,
2. Conjoint analysis.

A concept test is very straightforward: consumers are presented with a product idea and directly asked for their reaction (e.g., how likely would you be to buy this product?). We describe this type of testing and provide examples in Section I. While useful in many situations, the standard concept test has some important limitations. To a large extent, these limitations relate to the diagnostic information provided. If consumers collectively rate a product concept poorly, we know we should not launch the product—but the real question we want input to is how to fix it so that we do have a product that is acceptable to the marketplace. The consumer's reaction to a product (e.g., I am likely to buy it or I'm not) is a reflection of the consumer's underlying preferences.

Conjoint analysis, described in Section II, is a set of procedures developed to overcome a fundamental limitation of concept tests. In conjoint, we reorient our efforts not to look at reactions to a product idea per se but to get insight into the underlying preferences. The development of software to facilitate the consumer questioning and data analysis to achieve this result has been an active area of research—both by market research practitioners and academics. Conjoint is a staple of market research firms' offerings, and several firms specialize in conjoint applications. Thousands of conjoint studies are done each year in product categories ranging from hotels, rural health care systems, and cellular telephones to blue jeans. Section II describes this method and includes example applications. While not focusing on statistical details, we provide some intuition for the data analysis procedures.

---

Professor Robert J. Dolan prepared this note as the basis for class discussion.

## Section I: Concept Testing

Standard Concept Tests are widely used. For example, Colgate-Palmolive[1] faced the issue of whether or not to introduce a new toothbrush and how to position it. Research was conducted presenting mock advertisements conveying various positioning alternatives to consumers. Consumers reacted to the offerings on a five-point "purchase intention" scale, marking one box:

| | |
|---|---|
| Definitely would buy | ☐ |
| Probably would buy | ☐ |
| Might/Might not buy | ☐ |
| Probably would not buy | ☐ |
| Definitely would not buy | ☐ |

The best of the Colgate options found 87% of consumers rating the concept in one of the "top two boxes." This information helped to indicate the potential for the product.

In a similar vein, when BIOPURE[2] received FDA approval for a blood substitute for dogs, it conducted a survey in which the product was described to veterinarians who were then asked if they "would try" the product in critical and noncritical cases. At a price of $100, 95% reported being willing to try for critical cases and 70% for noncritical.

### *Executing a Concept Test*

Designing a concept test presents the usual survey design issues of what sample size to have and how to select respondents. In addition to this, the two key executional decisions in a concept test are

1. How to communicate the concept,
2. The data to collect from respondents.

On the first issue, Colgate chose to present a "positioning concept" (i.e., the product concept was presented in persuasive form by showing consumers mock advertisements for the Precision toothbrush). An alternative is to state the core idea only without an accompanying marketing message (e.g., "Precision is a new toothbrush with bristles of varying lengths resulting in 35% more plaque removal."). There is no general rule on "core idea" vs. "positioning concept" being the better choice for concept testing. Generally, using a "positioning concept" approach gives better prediction of actual marketplace reaction because there is a closer match of what the respondent sees to what will be seen in the actual purchase situation. The caveat on "positioning concepts" is that the response obtained is a reaction both to the product and the quality of the accompanying presentation

[1] "Colgate-Palmolive Company: The Precision Toothbrush," HBS Nos. 593-064 or 499-082 (condensed version).

[2] "BIOPURE Corporation," HBS No. 598-150.

of the positioning. So, two things are being mixed together. Another important point is not to be comparing scores from a "positioning concept" test and a "core idea" test.

The second issue is the data to collect. Colgate and BIOPURE typify concept testing in that some form of purchase intention data were collected. This is often augmented by three other forms yielding the set:

1. Intended Purchase Measures
2. Overall Product Diagnostics
3. Special Attribute Diagnostics
4. Respondents Profiling Variables

**Data Type #1: Purchase Measures** Purchase measures include likelihood of purchase and expected amount. Purchase intention is captured through questions like "Based on this product description, how likely would you be to buy this product if it were conveniently available?"; check one:

- ❑ Definitely would buy
- ❑ Probably would buy
- ❑ Might or might not buy
- ❑ Probably would not buy
- ❑ Definitely would not buy

While this five-point scale is most common, six-, seven-, and eleven- point scales are also used.

For nondurable goods, the frequency of purchase is also key. Purchase intent is a good indicator of trial, but forecasting volume sold requires knowing whether the product will be part of someone's everyday consumption habit or a special-occasion item. The expected purchase incidence question adds this dimension. Again, there is a variety of ways to specify this question but generally it takes a form such as "Which statement best describes how often you think you would buy this product if it were conveniently available to you?"

- Once a week or more often
- Once every two or three weeks
- Once a month
- Once every two to three months
- Once every four to six months
- Less often
- Never

In cases where the product may come in different sizes or is such that multiple units might be purchased at one time, respondents are probed on these issues as well.

In summary, given

Sales volume per potential user in time period = % of potential users in market who try product

* Expected number of purchases in the period for triers

* Expected number of units per purchase

the purchase measures from a concept test typically are designed to measure the three variables on the right-hand side.

**Data Type #2: Overall Product Diagnostics** Diagnostic data give insight into why the purchase data turned out the way it did. With respect to the overall concept, tests usually assess the product's perceived uniqueness (e.g., On a 1-5 scale where 1 = very similar and 5 = quite distinct, how would you rate the product relative to ones currently on the market?) and believability (i.e., Does the respondent believe the product can do what it claims?). For example, can the Colgate Precision toothbrush remove 35% more plaque?

Since a high-uniqueness, high-believability concept could still generate low purchase interest, firms usually assess how salient the product is to solving a consumer's problem and its overall interest to the consumer. For example, while a respondent may rate a television permitting the viewing of three channels at once as both unique and believable, purchase interest may be low because the respondent does not view the current channel constraint as a problem.

**Data Type #3: Specific Attribute Diagnostics** When a concept has a number of attributes or benefits offered, it is useful to probe which attributes/benefits significantly contribute to or distract from the purchase intention. One method is the use of open-ended questions such as "you said that you [state respondent's answer to purchase intention question]. What is it specifically about the product that makes you feel this way?"

A second approach is to collect data on perceptions of specific attributes and their importance to the consumer. For example, we might ask respondents exposed to a new Internet Service concept for data on perception and importance scales as follows:

**Perception: How do you perceive the service on each of the following dimensions?**

| | Excellent | | | | Poor |
|---|---|---|---|---|---|
| Entertainment Value | ☐ | ☐ | ☐ | ☐ | ☐ |
| Educational Value | ☐ | ☐ | ☐ | ☐ | ☐ |
| Ease of Site Navigation | ☐ | ☐ | ☐ | ☐ | ☐ |

| Attribute Importance: How important is the attribute to you? | Very Important | | | | Not at all important |
|---|---|---|---|---|---|
| Entertainment Value | ☐ | ☐ | ☐ | ☐ | ☐ |
| Educational Value | ☐ | ☐ | ☐ | ☐ | ☐ |
| Ease of Site Navigation | ☐ | ☐ | ☐ | ☐ | ☐ |

**Data Type #4: Respondents Profiling Variables** The final set of variables useful in analyzing concepts is the type of consumers who respond in different ways. The most obvious of these is demographics, which help in targeting efforts, but other more innovative data collection can be useful as well, for example, data on

- Current purchase behavior,
- Perception of the category,
- Satisfaction with current brands used,
- Influence in actual purchase decision.

For example, it might be important to understand how satisfied those with high purchase-intent scores are with their current brand. High satisfaction with the current brand makes a switch to a new brand less likely.

## *Interpreting the Purchase Intent Data*

The Purchase Intent score is at the heart of a concept test. How does one best interpret these data? Colgate Precision got an 87% "top-two box" score; is this good or bad? If the brush was introduced, what sales volume could Colgate expect? These are two important, logical questions.

General rules of thumb on "good" purchase-intent scores exist. For example, Taylor, Houlahan, and Gabriel[3] claim that, based on their experience with over 100 brands in many product categories, ". . . a concept statement should receive 80% to 90% favorable answers ["I definitely will buy" or "probably will buy"] to encourage subsequent development work." Schwartz[4] states the following average scores for concept tests across all product categories:

| | |
|---|---|
| Definitely will buy | 19% |
| Probably will buy | 64% |

Adding these two gives an 83% favorable rating score—a number not inconsistent with the rule-of-thumb of Taylor, Houlahan, and Gabriel. However, Schwartz also makes the important point that average scores vary appreciably across product categories. For example, he presents data on four categories' average "definitely will buy" scores as shown in **Figure A**.

[3] J. Taylor, J. Houlahan, and A. Gabriel, "The Purchase Intention Question in New Product Development: A Field Test," *Journal of Marketing*, January 1975, pp. 90-92.

[4] D. Schwartz, *Concept Testing*, AMACOM, 1987.

**Figure A** Average "definitely will buy" percent—Across all categories and in four specific categories

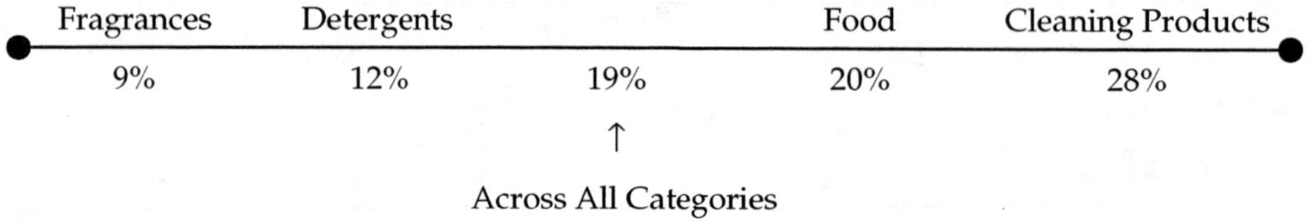


Thus, while Taylor et al.'s "rule-of-thumb" may be a useful first cut in assessing the "goodness" of the purchase intent scores, it is only that. The variation in scores across categories shows the need to have category specific norms or benchmarks. These norms can come from (i) published sources (such as Schwartz), (ii) the company's own files, or (iii) the files of the research company hired to do the concept test. Helpful information from published sources is very limited. The second source may suffice for an active company regularly introducing products into the same categories. Generally, however, there is important value in the benchmarks established by research firms with a broad array of clients participating in many product categories. BASES Worldwide, the largest concept testing firm, has done over 10,000 concept testings and hence has a valuable database to assist in interpreting results.[5]

## Section II: Conjoint Analysis

Concept tests have had a long history of use in marketing and continue to be a viable research option in many situations. Testing is relatively inexpensive, the results and methods are easily understood, and the benchmarks developed over time help in interpreting results.

However, in many situations today, the product design question is of a level of complexity that overruns the capabilities of the standard concept test. The issue is not how many people will intend to buy my 233 MHz personal computer, but how many more would be willing if I made it with 300 MHz? Suppose I had to charge $200 more for it? Suppose to offset the cost of speed, I downgrade the screen size? Made the product heavier? Reduce the warranty length? Conjoint analysis gives us a way to answer these critical questions. It has been used in a wide variety of product categories to deal with these issues of the augmented product design (i.e., product features and other value-adds like brand name and warranty coverage) and pricing. **Table A** presents a representative list.[6]

Of course, we can't get the insights conjoint provides for free. It is more difficult to develop an in-depth-enough understanding of the technique to be a responsible, productive user of it. It is more expensive and time consuming to do a conjoint study than a concept test. But, its record of successful use and its taking a place in the repertoire of first-rate marketers make exploration of it more than worthwhile.

The idea behind conjoint is simple. Think about a product category in which the hierarchy of effects is of the Learn→ Feel→ Do type (e.g., buying a new PC, enrolling in a health club, subscribing to an information service). In product categories with a high-cognitive front end, we often look at a

[5] P. Green, A. Krieger, T. Vavra, "Evaluating New Products," *Marketing Research*, Winter 1997.

[6] Drawn from R.J. Dolan, "Managing the New Product Development Process," HBS No. 592-011, and P. Green, *et al.*, "Evaluating New Products."

product as a bundle of attributes. An individual's "value system" is simply how much value the person would put on each level of the attributes. That's what we need to know to dig into the kind of questions noted above on how to trade features off against each other.

The problem is that if we walked up to a consumer and said, "Please tell me your value system," he or she probably could not do it even if they wanted to. In conjoint, we get around this by asking the consumer a series of questions he or she can more easily answer (e.g., which would you prefer: a Dell running at 233 MHz for $2,000 or a Packard-Bell, running at 300 MHz for $1,700?) and we let statistic procedures do the hard stuff (i.e., go from these answers to an estimate of the underlying "value system").

**Table A**

*Consumer Durables*

- Automobiles
- Cameras
- Cellular telephones
- Computers
- Condominium design and pricing
- Food processors
- Snowmobiles

*Consumer Nondurables*

- Blue jeans
- Rug cleaners
- Shampoos

*Consumer Services*

- Credit cards
- Rural health care systems
- Hotels
- Railway pricing

*Industrial Goods*

- Lift trucks
- Material requirements planning systems
- Copiers

The trick in conjoint is that, via construction of the value system, we bootstrap ourselves up from asking about preferences on a small subset of products to being able to make predictions about relative preference for *any* products with these attributes. This point will become clearer as we go along. First, we consider how one can calculate a "value system" from some overall judgments.

To get a sense of how it works, let's take an example. Consider a fitness facility interested in optimal design of its locker rooms. To keep things simple, let's say there are only two attributes potentially important to users: (i) whether or not there is a sauna and (ii) the size of available lockers. There are two alternative "levels" for the sauna ("yes" and "no") and three levels for lockers:

a. Small (20″ x 20″ x 20″) storage lockers permanently assigned plus large hanging ones (72″ x 20″ x 20″) for daily use.

b. Mid-size only (36″ x 20″ x 20″) permanently assigned.

c. No permanently assigned locker; hanging locker (72″ x 20″ x 20″) available on daily basis with mirror inside door.

There are thus 2 x 3 = 6 different sauna/locker combinations or products. One might in practice ask individuals how important these alternative attributes are. Alternatively, one can simply ask the respondent to rank order the 6 possible combinations from *most* to *least preferred*. The individual might respond as follows:

| | | Sauna: Yes | Sauna: No |
|---|---|---|---|
| | (SM) Small storage, large daily | Rank 2 | Rank 4 |
| **Locker** | (MED) Medium storage only | Rank 1 | Rank 3 |
| | (DAY) Large daily with mirror only | Rank 5 | Rank 6 |

With these ranks, we can ask the respondent to rate the desirability of the products, ranging from *least desirable* (a score of 0) to *most* (a score of 100). Suppose we are given the following ratings:

| | | Sauna: Yes | Sauna: No | |
|---|---|---|---|---|
| | SM | 80 | 40 | Average = 60 |
| **Locker** | MED | 100 | 60 | Average = 80 |
| | DAY | 20 | 0 | Average = 10 |
| | | Average = 66.7 | Average = 33.3 | |

Since each locker size is rated with both levels of the sauna attribute, we can calculate the utility of an attribute level as the average of the score across all choices where it appears. Following this, we would have:

**Sauna:**
Yes = 66.7
No = 33.3

**Locker:**
SM = 60
MED = 80
DAY = 10

This is the individual's "value system." Note that it recaptures the stated original ranking data:

| Product | Value System Score | Value System Score Rank | Stated Original Rank |
|---|---|---|---|
| MED + Sauna | 80 + 66.7 = 146.7 | 1 | 1 |
| SM + Sauna | 60 + 66.7 = 126.7 | 2 | 2 |
| MED + No Sauna | 80 + 33.3 = 113.1 | 3 | 3 |
| SM + No Sauna | 60 + 33.3 = 93.3 | 4 | 4 |
| DAY + Sauna | 10 + 66.7 = 76.7 | 5 | 5 |
| DAY + No Sauna | 10 + 33.3 = 43.3 | 6 | 6 |

With this value system, we can get an idea of how important the two attributes are to the consumer: the highest-rated locker option has 80 points and the lowest has 10 for a difference of 70. The sauna differential is only 33.3, suggesting the sauna attribute is less important than the locker attribute.

In practice, obviously, things are more complicated. We have lots more attributes and we use a multiple regression-type procedure to go from overall judgments to estimated value system. Conjoint is built on the idea of something called a part-worth model. It says, if a product in a category has *n* attributes, then the utility of an object *i* in the category is:

$$U_i = U_{i1} + U_{i2} + U_{i3} + \dots\dots\dots U_{in}$$

| ↑ | ↑ | ↑ |
|---|---|---|
| Utility of an object *i* to consumer | Utility of object *i*'s level of attribute #1 to consumer | Utility of object *i*'s level of attribute *n* to consumer |

That is, to get the utility of an item, we just sum up over all its attributes. The idea of conjoint is that consumers have a pretty good idea of the things on the left-hand side of the equation (i.e., we can ask them about that and use that pretty reliable information to estimate the stuff on the right-hand side).

Now we will go through a real application to see how it works in practice. This is an actual study[7] for a German automobile company to design and price its new model, code-named LION. LION would be positioned in the marketplace against models from two competitors—another German-based company and a Japanese company.

### *Step 1 Choose Attributes*

The first step in a conjoint study is to specify the possibly relevant attributes. Based on past research and its wealth of experience in the category, management specified five key attributes:

1. Brand name
2. Engine power
3. Fuel consumption
4. Environmental performance
5. Price

(A preliminary research stage is sometimes necessary to elicit possible relevant attributes from consumers, e.g., if this is a new product category for the firm.) Note the important capability that conjoint can handle a mix of hard, tangible features like engine power and fuel consumption, and intangibles like brand.

### *Step 2 Choose Relevant Levels of Attributes*

Determine the relevant levels of the attributes that consumers should be asked to evaluate. In this case, we specified the same number of levels (three) for each of the attributes. This need not be the case, however. Conjoint can accommodate any practical number of attribute levels for an attribute. The following attribute levels were used:

---

[7] This study was reported on in R.J. Dolan and H. Simon, *Power Pricing* (New York: Free Press, 1996).

- Brand
  - LION, "German" and "Japanese" (in the study, the actual names of the "German" and "Japanese" brands were used; but, for confidentiality reasons, we use those terms here)
- Engine Horsepower
  - 150 HP, 200 HP, and 250 HP
- Fuel Consumption
  - 12, 14, and 16 liters per 100 Km
- Environmental Performance
  - (i) fulfills minimum requirements, (ii) exceeds minimum requirements, and (iii) sets new standards in environmental performance
- Price (Deutschmarks/DM)
  - 50,000, 60,000, and 70,000

Respondents were given a detailed description of the Environmental Performance variable and the above listing is a shorthand representation.

### *Step 3 Choose a Sample Size and Respondent Type*

Respondents were prescreened for interest in buying an automobile in the 50,000 to 70,000 DM range within a specified time horizon.

### *Step 4 Choose Response Task and Survey Administration Mode*

In this case, a pairwise comparison approach was used. This method describes two alternatives on all five dimensions and asks the consumer for a preference judgment between the pair. The survey was administered on a laptop computer. An example screen is as follows:

| A | | B |
|---|---|---|
| *LION Brand* | | *Japanese Brand* |
| Fulfills minimum environmental requirements<br>Fuel consumption: 16 liters<br>Horsepower: 250<br>Price: DM 60,000 | OR | Exceeds environmental requirements<br>Fuel consumption: 12 liters<br>Horsepower: 150<br>Price: DM 50,000 |

If you prefer A, press A; if you prefer B, press B.

The alternatives are set up so the consumer has to trade off one thing to get another. On this screen, LION is markedly better than "Japanese" on Engine Power but performs in an inferior fashion on environmental standards, fuel consumption, and price. Depending on his or her preferences, the respondent makes a choice. The computer software then produces another choice to be made. Because the interview was done on a laptop, the program "learns" the consumer's preferences as it goes and so can adapt the questions to zero in on areas of uncertainty. Usually between 15 and 20 choice comparisons were needed to calibrate the underlying value system. Interview times varied between 30 and 60 minutes.

### *Step 5 Compute Individual Customer Value Systems*

A strong point of conjoint is that value systems are estimated at the level of the individual respondent. There is no presumption that respondents have the same value system. As such, conjoint can be a useful method for defining market segments based on differing attributes of importance.

### *Step 6 Analyze the Data*

**(a) Attribute Level Values** Often it is useful to look at average values of attributes across the full respondent set to get a general sense of the market.

**Table B** gives the results for this study. The five panels give the results for each attribute individually. For each attribute, the lowest scale value is 0. Vertical value scales are comparable across attributes.

**Table B** Values of Attribute Levels for LION Case

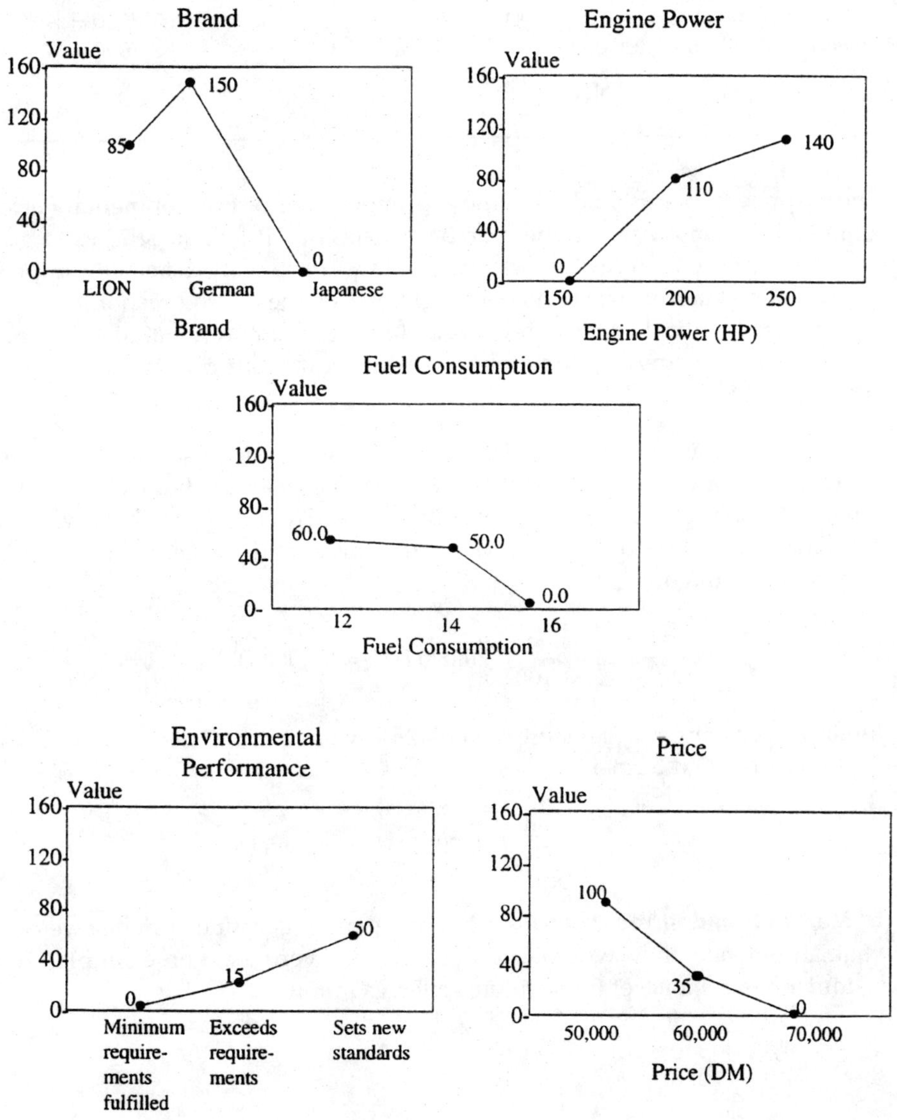

We can get a rough indicator of the relative importance of attributes by looking at the spread of the high-to-low values of the attribute. One has to be careful in interpreting this because the value obviously depends on the attribute levels we have chosen for the study. For example, if the Environmental Performance variable included an attribute level "Fails to Meet Requirements After First Year," that would drive up the value difference between lowest and highest attribute levels.

From the values in **Table B** we can derive a rough measure of attributes' importance.

| | **(1) Highest Score for any level of this Attribute** | **% of Importance = Col. (1) entry divided by Total of Col. (1)** |
|---|---|---|
| Brand | 150 | 150/500 = 30% |
| Engine Power | 140 | 140/500 = 28% |
| Price | 100 | 100/500 = 20% |
| Fuel Consumption | 60 | 60/500 = 12% |
| Environmental Performance | 50 | 50/500 = 10% |
| Total | 500 | |

One surprise from this study was the low importance of Environmental Performance, estimated at only 10% of the purchase decision. Previous studies done by the company featured surveys in which people were directly asked the importance of environmental performance. As one might expect, the offered response was typically that it was critical. Here, however, to "get" environmental performance, a respondent had to give up something else, like power or price, and was generally not inclined to do so.

Because price was one of the variables, one can get a rough sense of the dollar value (or actually DM value here) of different performance levels. For example, the "brand value" of LION over "Japanese" was 85 points. The price panel shows a 100-point difference equating to 20,000 DM. Thus, the brand value of LION relative to "Japanese" is roughly:

$$\frac{85}{100} * 20{,}000\text{ DM} = 17{,}000\text{ DM}$$

Similarly, reducing fuel consumption by 25%, from 16 to 12 liters per km, was worth 60 points, or in DM terms:

$$\frac{60}{100} * 20{,}000\text{ DM} = 12{,}000\text{ DM}$$

**(b) Market Simulations** Once we have respondents' value systems, we can predict what automobile they would choose from a given set. For example, suppose a customer had a choice of three automobiles, as follows:

| Attribute | Model A | Model B | Model C |
|---|---|---|---|
| • Brand | LION | German | Japanese |
| • Engine Power | 150 | 200 | 250 |
| • Fuel Consumption (liters/100km) | 12 | 16 | 14 |
| • Environmental Performance | new standards | meets requirements | meets requirements |
| • Price (DM) | DM 60,000 | DM 70,000 | DM 50,000 |

Let's assume this person's value system matched the average market system in **Table B.** Then, we can compute the value he or she would place on each option:

Model A: 230 value points (LION = 85 + Power = 0 + Fuel = 60 + Environmental = 50 + Price = 35)

Model B: 260 value points (by some method)

Model C: 290 value points (by some method)

Two rules are commonly used to translate value points into predictions of share. First is the simple "the consumer buys whatever is the highest point total." This is called the "Maximum Utility Rule." Using that rule, we would predict this person would buy Model C. We can look at part-worths to say this is due to its Engine Power. An alternative rule is the "Share of Utility" rule in which the probability of buying a given model is proportional to its value points, i.e.,

$$\textit{Probability Buy Model A} = 230/(230 + 260 + 290) = 29\%$$

Similarly, the probabilities for B and C would be 33% and 37% respectively.

Note that once we have the value system estimates for a representative set of individuals, we can simulate any scenarios we like, e.g.,

- What happens at various price points?
- What happens if LION is offered in two models?
    a. LION, 150 HP, 12 liters, New Standards, DM 60,000, and
    b. LION, 200 HP, 14 liters, Meets Requirements, DM 70,000

The first scenario of price changes was fully investigated in this study and the optimal price found to be DM 54,000 vs. DM 60,000 as originally intended, when the thinking was consumers were willing to pay for environmental performance.

## General Conjoint Decision Issues

There are a number of different approaches to conjoint, varying mostly in the task which is placed upon respondents. We saw one particular form in the LION study. Respondents were asked *pairwise preferences*. An offshoot of this is to ask the respondent "by how much" is one option preferred, e.g., "Press a number from 1 to 9 to indicate your preference where 1 represents you prefer option A a great deal, 5 if you are indifferent between the two options, and 9 means you prefer option B a great deal."

Another common approach is to take "full profiles" (i.e., ratings of objects on all the attributes in the study) and simply ask for an absolute rating of desirability rather than pairwise comparisons. Essentially this produces data similar to the pairwise preference methods; the key question is, what response task can a respondent do more reliably?

Finally, there is a hybrid method which uses one of the two methods above in conjunction with the respondents' own estimates—or "self-explicated" ratings. Lilien and Rangaswamy's software from *New Product and Brand Management*,[8] Chapter 4, follows this approach.

## Guidelines for Use

Conjoint is a powerful tool with broad applicability. Necessary assumptions underlying conjoint have been mentioned throughout this discussion. We collect them here to summarize situations wherein conjoint would be most applicable.

1. *Product as a Bundle of Attributes*

   The product must be able to be specified as a collection of attributes. There are some largely image products (e.g., a perfume) for which this is just not possible.

2. *Must Know Important Attributes*

   Conjoint requires that we either know or find out by another method what attributes are salient in the product category.

3. *Respondents Can Reasonably Rate Products*

   The input data we require from respondents are overall preference or purchase-likelihood judgments. This requires a level of respondent familiarity with the product category.

4. *Attributes Should be Actionable*

   The firm should, in most cases, be able to act upon the output of the conjoint by constructing products that deliver the attribute levels used in the analysis.

This note has tried only to communicate the basic principles of conjoint analysis. Many researchers are currently at work expanding the domain of applicability and accuracy of conjoint. Specialist market research firms exist to deal with complicated applications while straightforward ones can be addressed internally. State-of-the-art software is available inexpensively. Complicated or straightforward, effective use of conjoint requires that the manager understand the technique, its vast potential, and its limitations.

---

[8] G. Lilien and A. Rangaswamy, *New Product and Brand Management: Marketing Engineering Applications* (Reading, Mass.: Addison Wesley, 1999).

## DISCOVERING WHAT HAS ALREADY BEEN DISCOVERED: WHY DID YOUR CUSTOMERS HIRE YOUR PRODUCT?

(C. Christensen / #9-699-029 / 9p)

### Summary

Describes a methodology for identifying markets for new technologies and for defining the highest value attributes of new products or services. It helps innovators escape the trap of incremental improvements to established product concepts by asking a straightforward question: What job did my customer hire this product to do for him or her?

### Outline

Discovering What the Customer Has Discovered: The Case of Baking Soda
Obviating the Need to Change Customer Behavior
Finding Innovative Product Ideas Using the Jobs-to-be-Done Framework
An Example of Discovering What Customers Discovered: Milkshakes for Breakfast
Conclusion

### Learning Objectives

- Understand shortcomings of traditional market research in fueling innovation.
- Acquire a practical tool for identifying breakthrough new product ideas and market applications.

### Questions, Ideas, and Exercises

1. It's possible that your customers have already discovered new applications for your company's products. How would you know if they did? Assess the strength and diversity of the information channels through which you might acquire such information. Are you seeking this information proactively from salespeople, distributors, customer service representatives, or retail workers? Do you have, or could you develop, the technological capability to "eavesdrop" on customers as Intuit did in the Quickbooks example?

2. The Quickbooks example identifies a trap into which market researchers and product developers are apt to fall: focusing on the addition of features and functionalities to a product that the customer actually wants simplified. Is this a trap into which you have fallen with any of your own products? Do you have good information about which product features most of your customers are *not* using?

# Discovering What Has Already Been Discovered: Why Did Your Customers Hire Your Product?

Executives and market researchers with responsibility for finding better ideas for more innovative new products and services are constantly developing more sophisticated methods for listening to their customers and understanding what unfulfilled customer needs they might address next. An entire profession has arisen around techniques for assembling focus groups that represent targeted customer segments, and for asking the right questions to elicit subtle and hitherto unexpressed needs. Habits and attitudes surveys which chart major behavioral and demographic trends often constitute the foundation for the long-term strategies of consumer products companies. And once best-practice market researchers have determined what features or attributes their customers need in next-generation products, good product designers have rigorous methods to ensure that the necessary attributes are integrated into the product's design, and that the proper trade-offs are made.[1] State-of-the-art techniques for assessing consumers' reactions to advertisements, or for defining the meaning of brands in consumers' minds, can actually measure changes in the patterns of blood flow in the brain, as subjects see different images or hear different words and sounds.[2]

Although these methods yield valuable insight and consumer understanding, most executives remain dissatisfied with the true creativity of their staffs' efforts to develop and introduce innovative new products and services. Descriptors such as *unexciting, me-too*, and *flop* are used much more commonly in reviews of product development performance than words such as *breakthrough, ingenious*, and *on-target*. Why? One reason, of course, is that understanding what does not exist is a genuinely difficult business. But another possibility is that market researchers often frame the problem they are trying to understand in the wrong terms: they look at customers and market structures from their *own* perspective, rather than seeking to understand how the customer sees the world.

Most companies organize the measurement of their markets and define the boundaries of their business in terms of product categories and/or technological competencies. For example, margarine is a product category. There are margarine manufacturers and margarine brands, and there is margarine space in supermarket cabinets. Margarine manufacturers measure their success by how rapidly they are causing the margarine category to grow, and by what share of the category they are able to capture. Mayonnaise is another product category, made in different kinds of factories, marketed under different brands, and placed in a different place in the supermarket. Almost anyone

*Professor Clayton Christensen prepared this note as the basis for class discussion rather than to illustrate either effective or ineffective handling of an administrative situation. The assistance of Richard Pedi of Pedi-Moesta Associates, and Julia Wesson of PataleX are gratefully acknowledged.*

working in a company making margarine or mayonnaise would assure you that margarine is indeed a *very* different business than mayonnaise. And from their point of view, they are assuredly right.

But are categories of products and services really the way that *customers* view the world? To some extent, of course, they do see the world this way -- because suppliers have trained them. Most consumers would repeat back to a market researcher that margarine is a different product category than mayonnaise because they are branded differently and sold in different locations. But at the point of use, most customers employ a very different view of the world. They have a job that needs to be done, and they search across multiple product categories to find something that does that job as effectively as possible.

For example, a parent rushing to make sandwiches for school lunches in the morning has a job to be done. The child won't eat the sandwich for several hours, and if the bread is dry around the edges the child will have a hard time swallowing it. So the parent looks around the kitchen for something to do the "moisten bread at the edges quickly" job. Spreading butter on the bread could do it, but butter wouldn't do this particular job as well as soft-tub margarine: spreading cold butter on soft bread takes time and rips the bread. Cream cheese could also do the job. And how about mayonnaise? Mayonnaise is easy to distribute around the edges of the bread that need moistening the most. A layer of lettuce might provide sufficient moistening, especially if the sandwich is sealed in a plastic pouch. While manufacturers are busy boasting about the superior flavor, texture, and fat content of their products compared to competitors *within* their categories, the consumer is busy scanning *across* categories for something that will do the job the best.

Looking at the market structure in terms of the types of jobs that different sets of customers need to have done, can lead innovating companies to very different assessments of who their competitors are; of the strengths and weaknesses of their products; of trends in their market shares; and of the types of changes in the features and functions of their products that customers are likely to value.[3]

But most importantly, working to understand the purposes for which customers pull products or services into their lives can change the fundamental character of the search for creativity. In essence, it frames market and consumer research as a quest *to discover what the customer has already discovered*. Customers are ingenious and inventive. When they have a job that needs to get done, they rarely let the job fester and languish, undone. They look around, find something that allows them to get by, and solve their problem. Often, they may not be solving the problem well -- frequently they are not even aware of the awkward ways in which they have adapted products that had been designed for other purposes, to do other jobs that needed to be done. Because of this, customers often are unable to articulate many dimensions of the jobs that they hire products to do for them. The hiring patterns, and the full reasoning behind them, can only be discovered through careful observation and analysis of what customers actually *do* with the products they buy.

## Discovering What the Customer Has Discovered: The Case of Baking Soda

For years, Church and Dwight Company supplied its Arm & Hammer brand baking soda in the baking supplies shelves of supermarkets -- a nice, profitable market niche which it dominated. There wasn't much to do in product development or market research: consumers' recipes either called for baking soda, or they didn't. But in contrast to Church and Dwight's somnolent pace of innovation, some of its customers were being marvelously innovative. Their refrigerators tended to retain smells, which tainted the taste of new foods stored in them. Homemakers had looked around for a product to solve this problem for them, and hired baking soda to do this job. Carpets likewise tended to accumulate old musty smells, and needed to be refreshed. Sometimes, homemakers would rent a carpet shampooer to do this job; sometimes they would hire a carpet cleaning service; and sometimes they would employ baking soda. Similarly, consumers who wanted a clean, zingy feeling in their mouths after eating had long employed baking soda to do the job -- sometimes creating custom toothpastes by putting toothpaste on a wet toothbrush, and then dipping it into a box of baking soda.

Church and Dwight found significant growth opportunities in deodorizers and toothpastes when it discovered what consumers had already discovered. Once it understood the purposes for which consumers were adapting Arm & Hammer brand baking soda for use in their lives, it framed a very different set of competitors. It became obvious which attributes of standard baking soda needed to be changed, so that baking soda could do each of the various jobs better than any of the competing solutions. And the company's branding and advertising strategies could become much clearer, once its managers grew to view the world from the consumer's point of view.

## Obviating the Need to Change Customer Behavior

Seeking to understand customers from a jobs-to-be-done perspective resolves another dilemma that has long plagued innovators: enticing consumers to change their behavior in order to use a "better" product. When a new product is designed with the attributes that enable it to perform even better in a job that customers have already been hiring it to do, they don't have to change their behavior. When customers have become accustomed to awkwardly "porting over" a product that was designed for another purpose to do the job at hand, and then find a product that does the job better, they are delighted. It is an easy sell.

Intuit is a company that has habitually structured its market research efforts to understand the world from its customers' point of view, rather than the supplier's point of view. It is famous for having followed customers home (with permission, of course) after they purchased the company's *Quicken®* personal finance software. Intuit's customer researchers would sit in the background, observing exactly what happened when customers installed and began to use *Quicken®*. This helped them make the product progressively more convenient and intuitive to use. It also helped them understand what *jobs* these customers were hiring *Quicken®* to do for them.

In the early 1990s, Intuit researchers observed that some *Quicken®* customers were using the product to handle the accounting for small businesses they managed. As the researchers worked to understand why the customers had hired *Quicken®* for this job rather than one of the plethora of small business accounting software packages in the market, they began to see why. The other small business software packages had been designed by accountants for accountants. The sorts of jobs that most accountants hire accounting software to do include analyzing depreciation schedules, aging accounts receivable; analyzing variances; and so on. But these small businesspeople had much simpler jobs to be done: they needed to know how much cash they had, and they needed to write checks. Not much more than that. Most of them wanted to feel like they were in control of their business; yet they knew little and cared less about the conventions of accounting, and did not employ a bookkeeper or accountant.

Guided by this understanding of the job that these customers had been hiring *Quicken®* to do, Intuit's developers created a new small business accounting software product, *Quickbooks®*, which was exquisitely convenient and which had exactly the features and functions needed to do the job for which unsophisticated small business owners had been hiring a sub-optimal solution. *Quickbooks®* had none of the sophisticated report generation capabilities of competing products, and yet it captured 80% of the small business accounting software market within two years.

## Defining the Exploration Space

How did the established accounting software players miss something that, in retrospect, seemed so obvious? **Exhibit 1**, which charts on its axes two important dimensions of innovation, suggests a reason: by viewing the exploration space from their own point of view, these companies had begun their search for next-generation products with an answer that was pre-determined. This condemned them, over and over again, to finishing their attempts to be innovative by introducing products that were more of the same, but a little better.

The vertical axis of Exhibit 1 depicts the alternative ways that researchers can express the benefit that a customer is seeking. At the bottom extreme, the researcher expresses the customer's benefit in terms specific to a product category -- such as, "Customers want a better accounting software package." At the other extreme, the researcher frames it in terms of a job to be done -- such as, "Customers need to write checks and keep track of cash balances without having to learn accounting." Researchers who frame their task at the bottom of the matrix are framing the business from the supplier's point of view. Researchers who frame the problem at the top of the matrix are better able to see the options from the customer's perspective, and therefore have more scope for creativity in innovation.

**Exhibit 1: The Exploration Space**

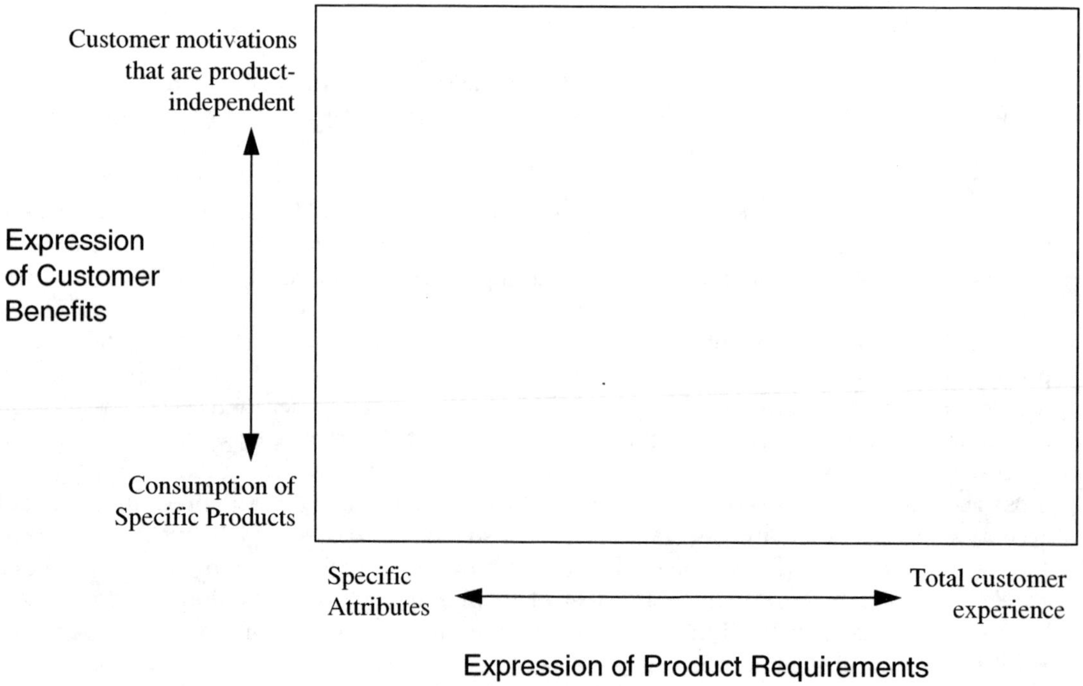


The horizontal axis of Exhibit 1 describes options for framing the customer's potential experience. At the left extreme, consumer research consists of assessing alternative product attributes: "Would you like your software package to be able to generate this kind of report? Would you like the meat on this hamburger to be thicker? Have less fat?" At the right extreme, in contrast, researchers seek to understand the complete experience that the customer has in buying and using the product, without assuming a particular technological solution or business approach for providing that experience.[4] Researchers who frame their task at the right side of this spectrum will have greater flexibility in designing a new product or service that gives the customer the complete experience -- in its physical, emotional, social and intellectual dimensions -- that will do the job for which the product is meant to be hired. We call the possibilities in the matrix defined by these two axes the "exploration space."

Too many innovators begin and end their search for consumer understanding and new product ideas in the lower-left corner of this map. When researchers begin by asking questions like "Would you prefer less fat in the margarines you buy?" they are likely to recommend introducing even lower-fat margarines. If researchers begin by asking "How did you feel when you last left a low-fat margarine on the kitchen counter over night, and opened the tub to find that the water had separated out of the margarine?" they are likely to conclude that the R&D department must come up with a way of making oil-and-water emulsions more stable at higher temperatures. Good ideas, these are. But the new products that result are unlikely to create breakthrough excitement in the marketplace.

In the case of small business accounting software noted above, the initial software packages that were available in the mid-1980s were quite simple. It is likely, however, that the market researchers for those companies kept asking their best customers questions such as, "What other features could you use in your accounting software products? Would you switch vendors if one provided options for these additional analyses and reports?" They started and ended their customer research in the lower left corner of the exploration space mapped in Exhibit 1 -- assuming that more features were better. As a result, generation after generation, the available products became increasingly complex, and it became difficult to differentiate among competitive offerings, each of which claimed to have the latest and greatest new features. It was only by carefully watching *what* the customers were actually doing, and seeking to understand *why* they were doing it -- by moving to the upper-right area of the innovation space -- that Intuit was able to break open the market with its *Quickbooks*® product.

## Finding Innovative Product Ideas Using the Jobs-to-be-Done Framework

**Exhibit 2** outlines how researchers can use the Jobs-to-Be-Done framework to innovate more effectively. The first step is to find customers who have recently purchased a product. It is important that they have actually purchased it, because customers' actions are a clearer indicator of their values and priorities than are verbally expressed intentions. Through carefully asking and watching, researchers can understand the circumstances the customer was in when he or she purchased and used the product -- they need to discover the job for which the product was hired. As shown in Exhibit 2, this step takes the researcher from the lower-left to the upper-left area of the exploration space.

In the second step, the researcher needs to understand the circumstances under which, and the reasons why, the customer recently may have purchased *different* products or services to do this same job. This helps in several ways. First, it helps the researcher define the job more sharply. Second, it helps define the set of products against which they are competing, in that particular job space. And most importantly, there are many dimensions of a customer's experience with a product, besides simply utilizing it, which define the social and emotional aspects of the job that needs to be done.[5] Understanding the functional, social, emotional motivations for hiring the product not only improves the researcher's understanding of the job to be done, but defines the total product experience required to do that job perfectly. It also helps the researcher understand the strengths and weaknesses of the *real* set of competing products, which on occasion get hired to do the particular job.

In completing step two, the researcher has essentially moved to the upper right corner of the exploration space -- having defined the job to be done in terms that are independent of any specific product or technology, and having defined the total experience required, independent of any specific product attributes. We call these definitions an "innovation specification." The innovation specification defines what the product must *do,* in order to satisfy the customer completely when he or she hires it.

**Exhibit 2: Developing and Using an Innovation Specification**

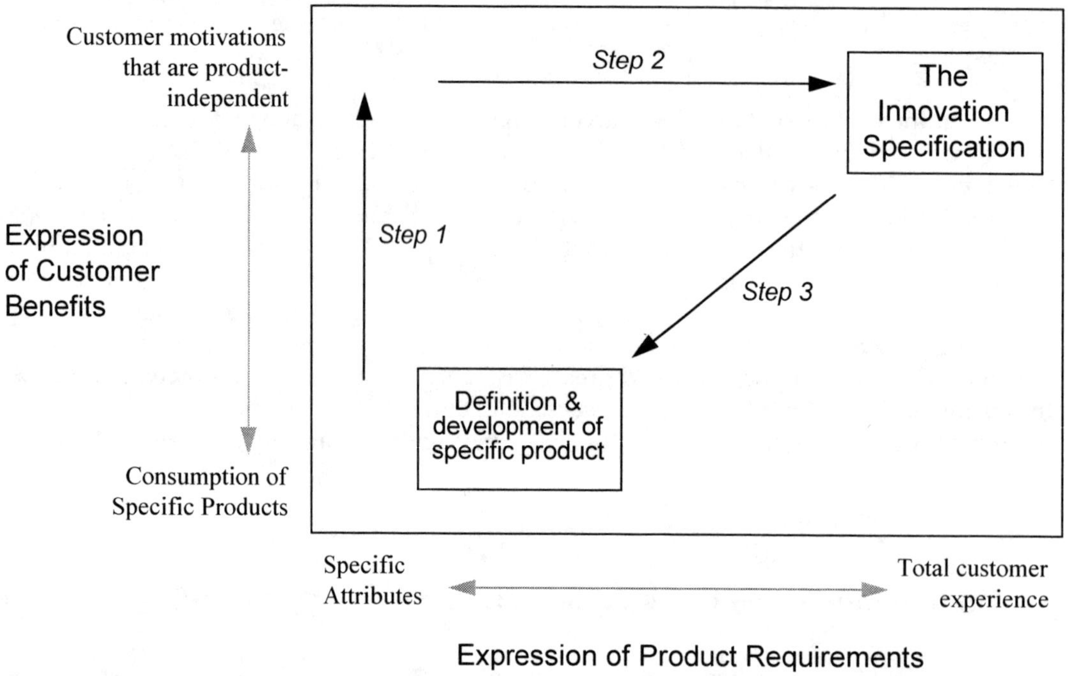


Armed with the directives in the innovation specification, an integrated product development team can then undertake step three -- moving back to the lower-left corner of the exploration space, to search for the particular technologies, product designs and attributes that are needed to deliver on that job. These developments include not just the physical product, of course, but also innovations in advertising, distribution, brand positioning, service and sales support, in order to create the required total product experience.

## The Value of Assessing Attributes in the Context of an Innovation Specification

Too often, market researchers ask customers to evaluate attributes of new products and innovations in the marketing mix, in a context that is divorced from the job for which the product or service is being hired to do. For example, if a television manufacturer asked me in a shopping mall consumer focus group whether I would be willing to pay more for a television screen that has much clearer resolution than the one on presently own, I probably would say the sharper image was important to me. If he asked whether I would pay a price premium for a set that would automatically change channels when I called out the channel number, I would also likely respond that I'd pay it.

But if the researcher actually watched to understand the jobs that I hire a television to do for me, he would note two hiring patterns. Most frequently, I hire television to get caught up on the news at zero net time cost, while I am washing dishes or doing the family ironing. The researcher would note my repeated frustration when I have to balance the iron on end and walk over to the television in order to switch to another news network, when the one I've been watching starts dwelling on topics of disinterest. For this job, a voice-activated channel switcher would delightfully satisfy my job to be done. A higher-resolution screen would be worth little, since I rarely look at the screen for longer than a few seconds anyway. The other job for which I hire television is to become intensely and enjoyably involved in big sporting events, such as the NCAA final four. For that job, visual clarity is enormously important, while voice-actuated channel switching is not.

If the television researcher developed a product based on the out-of-context shopping mall inputs noted above, his company would likely introduce a product with a clearer screen *and* voice-activated channel changing. It would be a costly, one-size fits all product that in some way dissatisfied me in both of the jobs for which I hired it. In the early years of television when consumers could afford only one set, this "averaging" approach was probably sensible. But in today's home with multiple televisions, drawing an average line through the differences in jobs only creates meaningless and confusing differentiation from the consumer's point of view.

In contrast to this approach of evaluating attributes in the absence of the job-to-be-done context, a innovation specification developed in the upper right region of Exhibit 2 can guide those who are evaluating different product concepts or features, or are piecing together various other elements of the marketing mix. It helps developers make sensible trade-offs, because they can juxtapose any proposal against the elements of the total product experience that are required to do the job.

## Jobs and the Meaning of Brands

Although it is the subject of ongoing research, we believe that when a manufacturer's branding strategy positions a "purpose" brand squarely and unambiguously upon the primary job for which the manufacturer wants customers to hire the product or service, the brand almost invariably has enormous power. For example, Sony's Walkman® brand is positioned squarely upon a job to be done -- providing a relaxing escape through private, mobile music. Sony, through its purpose brand Walkman®, <u>*owns*</u> this job. When customers hire a product to do this job for them, they immediately think of Walkman -- even if they eventually hire a "Walkman" made by Toshiba. Sony can extend its Walkman® brand to other products that are meant to be hired to do the same job -- as it did with its Diskman®. But if Sony attempted to extend this brand to products that are hired to do other jobs -- such as boom boxes -- it would confuse the customer.

Most brand architectures are *not* structured to help customers link the product with the job for which the product is meant to be hired. Instead, the marketers' goal seems to have been to position the product to be used in as many jobs as possible. The unfortunate result of this is that both the product and the brand are sub-optimized for every job. This confuses customers, and manufacturer that follow such branding strategies rarely dominate any category.

## An Example of Discovering What Customers Discovered: Milkshakes for Breakfast

A fast food restaurant chain recently used the jobs-to-be-done framework to reverse what had been a steady decline in the revenues and profitability of its milk shake product line. For years it had tried to improve milk shake sales and profits by focusing on the product. In consumer panels they explored whether making the shakes more chocolatey, thicker, cheaper, richer, or chunkier would reverse the product's fortunes. But even though many of the proposed product features met with a positive consumer response during the research phase, none of the new products significantly altered sales or profits.

Researchers for the chain then spent a full 18-hour day in a restaurant, carefully watching who bought milkshakes -- recording for each customer data such as time of purchase; what other products he or she purchased at the same time; whether the customer was alone or with a group; whether he or she consumed it on the premises, or drove off with it in the car; and so on. The most surprising insight from this work was that fully one-third of all milk shakes were bought in the morning, for *breakfast*.

The researchers came back on another day, and interviewed the customers who purchased a morning milk shake, to understand what they were going to do with it. They also asked what other products they purchased instead of a milk shake, when they had the same need. It turned out that most of these morning milk shake customers had hired it to do the same job. They had left for work late, didn't have time for breakfast, and needed to eat in the car to get to work on time. They had a long, boring commute. They weren't yet hungry, but knew that if they didn't eat something now, they'd be hungry by 10:00. This was the job that needed to be done.

When these customers looked around, it turned out that the milk shake did the job better than almost any available alternative. Sometimes they hired bagels, but bagels got crumbs all over their clothes and the car -- especially messy if they had cream cheese on them. Sometimes they hired a banana to do the job, but it got eaten too fast and didn't solve the boring commute problem. The sorts of sausage, ham or egg sandwiches that the restaurant also sold for breakfast made their hands and ultimately the steering wheel greasy. Donuts didn't last through the 10:00 hunger attack. But milk shakes could be eaten cleanly with one hand, with no risk of spillage. Their thick viscosity meant that they took a long time to eat; and the customers felt less hungry after eating the shake than after using the alternatives. They weren't quite satisfied that the shake was as healthy as a breakfast should be, but at least it had some milk in it.

Once the researchers understood the job that customers were hiring the shake to do in the morning, and understood the multiple dimensions of the product experience, the researchers were then able to define a new product that did an even better job. They swirled in chunks of real fruit -- which made it healthier and more interesting to eat. They made it even thicker, so it would last longer. And they served it with an especially thick straw, so the fruit chunks could be drawn through it. They gave it a new brand name and advertising campaign that focused not the product's physical attributes, but the job that they wanted consumers to associate with it. In the markets in which the new product has been launched, it has been *very* successful -- not because it captured milk shake sales from competing fast food chains, but because it captured a much larger share of the job, from products in other categories that periodically had been hired with limited satisfaction for this particular breakfast job.[6]

## Conclusion

There are many methods for searching for innovative new product and service ideas. While each has its strengths and weaknesses, in our experience most senior managers' assessment is that the weaknesses of many methods outweigh their strengths. We believe that a fundamental, underlying cause of the weakness in so many innovation efforts is that innovators' view of customers, markets and competitors is formed from the supplier's perspective. They have not worked to define the world in the ways that customers see it. In our experience, trying to understand what jobs customers hire particular products and services to do for them is a method that has a much higher probability of creating exciting, market share-changing new products and services – because when it is executed correctly, it focuses innovators on developing precisely the attributes and functionality that address the precise job that the customers need to have done.

---

[1] See, for example, Clausing, Don, "The House of Quality," *Harvard Business Review,*

[2] Professor Gerald Zaltman of the Harvard Business School has been a pioneer in developing consumer research techniques such as this.

[3] In many ways, our urging market researchers to take the customer's view of the world is reminiscent of Professor Ted Levitt's classic article, "Marketing Myopia," *Harvard Business Review,*

[4] If, for example, convenience in buying, installing and using a product is an important dimension of the job to be done, an attribute-specific framing of the task might be to provide a simpler, clearer user manual. A description of the *experience* required to do the job, in contrast, would broaden the innovator's search to include toll-free telephone numbers; having service personnel perform the installation and training on-site; or by creating simple, unambiguous product designs.

[5] As an example of what can be learned through this line of inquiry, imagine a customer (call her Julia), who tells a researcher that while she typically uses low-fat margarine to make her daughter's school lunch sandwiches. She occasionally uses mayonnaise, however, because *her* mother often used mayonnaise in making school lunch sandwiches when *she* was a little girl. Julia's mother was a good mother; and using mayonnaise on *her* daughter's sandwiches makes Julia feel like a good mother, too. Feelings such as Julia's are often a very important dimension of the job to be done.

[6] Many of the aspects of this project have been disguised in this account, to protect the proprietary interests of the company.

## NOTE ON BEHAVIORAL PRICING

(J. Gourville / #9-599-114 / 12p)

### Summary

Introduces the behavioral or psychological aspects of consumer price acceptance. Reviews the traditional economic approach to consumer price acceptance and explains shortcomings of that approach. Introduces the concept of transaction fairness. The behavioral side to product pricing is explored and eventually combined with elements of the traditional approach to produce a more realistic understanding of how consumers respond to a firm's pricing decisions.

### Outline

Purpose of this Note
Value Pricing and the Economic Perspective
Adding a Behavioral Component to the Economic Perspective
Some Behavioral Updates to the Economic Perspective
Managing Perceptions of Transaction Fairness
Summary

### Learning Objectives

- Understand the potential impact of certain behavioral variables on a consumer's willingness to pay an established price.
- Learn principles of managing price expectations and perceptions of costs of goods sold.

### Questions, Ideas, and Exercises

1. On the first page of this note, the author notes the results of a survey of managers regarding potential factors in product pricing decisions; only about one-fifth of the respondents felt well-informed about consumers' willingness to pay at various price levels. How aware of this dimension are the managers responsible for pricing decisions in your firm? Would they be interested in undertaking a program to obtain better consumer information of this type?

2. Consider Strategy #1 outlined on the next-to-last page of the note. Do you understand what reference prices your customers use for comparison with your prices? To what extent are customers taking their signals from your own product's pricing history versus competitors' prices? Are you taking proactive steps to manage price perception if you suspect customers may be viewing your pricing in a biased way? How well have you prepared colleagues who interface directly with customers to combat faulty pricing perceptions?

3. Review Strategy #2 on managing customers' perception of cost of goods sold. Consider making this issue an objective of your next market research project. Find out how customers perceive your cost of goods and the basis of their perceptions.

# Note on Behavioral Pricing

It is important for a firm to get its pricing "right." Consider the impact of product pricing on a firm's net income. If Coca-Cola could increase its prices by an average of 1%, without affecting consumer demand for its products, it would increase its net income by 6.4%. A price increase of less than 1¢ on a can of cola would translate to an increase in net income of about $300 million.

Similar 1% price increases, if they did not negatively impact demand, would lead to increases in net income of 16.7% for Fuji Photo, 17.5% for Nestle, and 26% for the Ford Motor Company. In fact, an average price increase of 1% would boost the net income of the typical large U. S. corporation by about 12%.[1]

These examples highlight the potential impact on a firm's net income of optimally setting product prices — small changes in price can have an enormous impact on income. Before raising (or lowering) prices in an attempt to improve the bottom line, however, a firm must understand and anticipate a consumer's response to a product price change.

Unfortunately, it appears that many firms lack the necessary understanding of a consumer's "willingness to pay" to optimally set product prices. When asked whether they were "well-informed" on six of the potential inputs to the product pricing decision, managers at one well-respected U.S.-based multinational responded as follows:[2]

- 84% were well-informed on the variable cost of providing their product.
- 81% were well-informed on the fixed cost of providing their product.
- 75% were well-informed on the price of competitors' products.
- 61% were well-informed on the value of their product to the customer.
- 34% were well-informed on how consumers would respond to price changes.
- 21% were well-informed on consumers' willingness to pay at various price levels.

These managers were well-informed on the costs of providing its products and on the price of competitor's products. They were also well-informed on the value its products delivered to consumers. However, when it came to a consumer's willingness to pay or to a consumer's response

---

1 From Robert J. Dolan and Hermann Simon's, *Power Pricing*, The Free Press, New York, NY (1995)

2 Ibid.

*Assistant Professor John T. Gourville prepared this note as the basis for class discussion rather than to illustrate either effective or ineffective handling of an administrative situation.*

to potential price changes, these managers were lacking the insight needed to optimally set prices. Experience suggests that this company is not unique in this regard.

## Purpose of this Note

Any firm's ability to optimally set product prices is governed by many factors. Some of these factors are well understood and are routinely incorporated into a firm's pricing decisions. These factors tend to be heavily weighted toward those economic factors that are easily obtained by a firm, including their own variable and fixed costs of production, the market price of competitors' products and the firm's internal assessment of the value that their product delivers to the intended consumer. Not surprisingly, these are the four factors on which the surveyed managers claimed that they were well-informed. We will briefly review these factors in a moment. [3]

However, optimal product pricing also hinges on a consumer's willingness to pay and on a consumer's response to price changes, factors on which the surveyed managers claimed they were poorly informed. In addition, research has shown that a consumer's willingness to pay is often influenced by "psychological" or "behavioral" variables that typically are not considered when setting price. Specifically, consumers often are as concerned with the behavioral question of "how fair a deal am I getting" as they are with the economic question of "how good a deal am I getting."

This note is an attempt to highlight the potential impact of some of these behavioral variables on a consumer's willingness to pay. In the process, it provides a more complete picture of consumer response to pricing and provides some insight for optimal product pricing.

## Value Pricing and the Economic Perspective

The traditional economic approach to product pricing is driven by a small handful of factors, as shown in **Figure A**. One of these factors is the "objective value" the product delivers to the consumer. [4] This is a measure of the benefits that the product delivers to the consumer, regardless of whether the consumer recognizes those benefits. When 61% of managers claim they are well-informed on the value of their product to the consumer, they are most likely referring to this "objective value."

A second factor in the economic approach to pricing is the "perceived value" of the product to a consumer. Perceived value is the value the consumer understands the product to deliver. Sometimes, a product's benefits are readily apparent to the consumer and "perceived value" approaches "objective value" with little effort by the firm. Other times, a product's benefits are less obvious and need to be communicated by the firm to the consumer (e.g., via advertising, personnel selling). In such cases, the "perceived value" of a product typically falls below its "objective value."

The perceived value of a product also can be influenced by the price of competing products or "substitutes." Company A may develop a product that creates great objective value for consumers. Consumers may recognize this value and be willing to pay a high price to obtain the product.

---

[3] For a more complete discussion of these economic factors, you should refer to Professor Corey's "Note on Pricing" [HBS Note #580-091] or Professor Dolan's "Pricing Policy" note [HBS Note #585-044].

[4] Given consumer heterogeneity, "objective value" and "perceived value" will tend to vary across consumers. For some consumers, these values will be high, for others, they will be low or zero. For simplicity, we will ignore consumer heterogeneity in this note and only consider the "typical" consumer. Nevertheless, the behavioral perspective offered in this note apply equally well to a heterogeneous consumer population.

However, if Company B introduces an identical product at a much lower price, the perceived value of Company A's product would be reduced to the price of Company B's product.

It is important to note that the "perceived value" of a product to a consumer *should* equal the maximum price that consumer is willing to pay for the product. Imagine a consumer who perceives the value of a modem to be $100. If priced above $100, the consumer has no incentive to buy the modem. If priced at $100 or less, however, the consumer always stands to gain from purchasing.

**Figure A** Value Pricing and the Economic Perspective

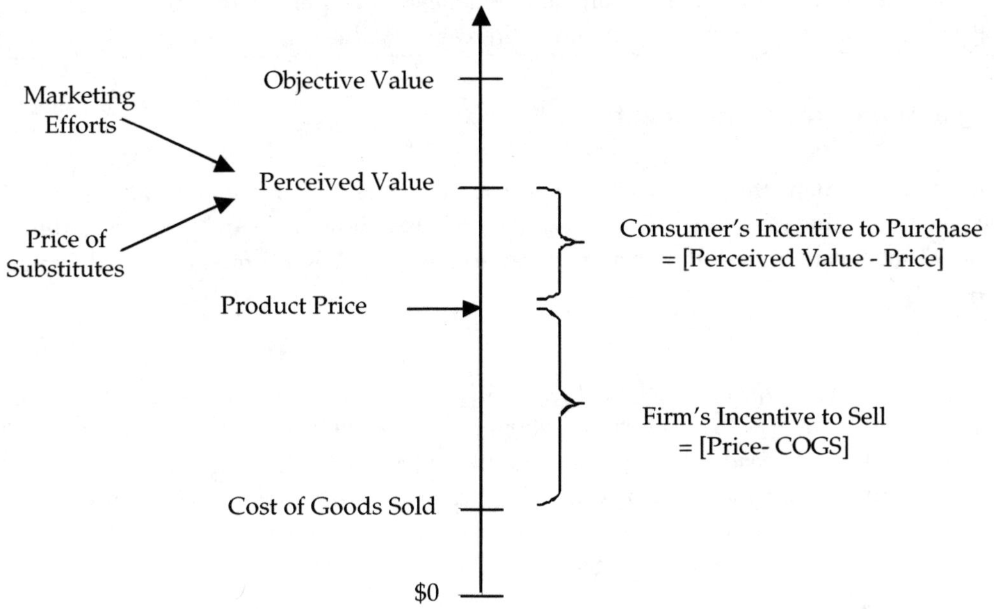


The last major component to the economic approach to pricing involves the firm's cost of goods sold (i.e., COGS). Just as the consumer requires an incentive to purchase a product, the firm requires an incentive to sell the product. In order to stay in business and make a positive return, a firm must charge a price that covers both its cost of production. [5]

All of these economic factors come together to form the "value pricing" approach to pricing. In optimally pricing a product, a firm is bound at the upper end by the consumers' "perceived value" for the product. This "perceived value" is influenced by the "objective value" of the product to the consumer, by the firm's marketing effort to communicate that objective value, and by the price of substitute products. At the same time, the firm is bound on the lower end by its COGS.

By pricing above COGS and below perceived value, the firm has an incentive to sell the product, measured as [price – COGS], and the consumer has an incentive to purchase the product, measured as [perceived value – price]. In value pricing terminology, the firm has "created" value by offering a product that the consumer values at a price greater than the firm's COGS. In turn, by pricing between perceived value and COGS, the firm has "captured" some of that value for itself and has allowed consumers to capture the remainder.

---

5 For simplicity, we will ignore strategic reasons for pricing below cost such as to build share or volume or to temporarily respond to a competitor's pricing efforts.

## Adding a Behavioral Component to the Economic Perspective

This "value pricing" framework provides a basic model of how an economically rational consumer *should* respond to a firm's pricing of a product. A rational consumer *should* purchase a product as long as the "perceived value" of that product is greater than the actual price being charged. In addition, the more one's perceived value exceeds actual price, the greater should be a consumer's incentive to buy. This leads to the fairly straight forward claim that:

**The Economic Perspective: Consumers Buy When Perceived Value Exceeds Price**

Consumers should purchase an item whenever the perceived value of that item exceeds its actual price [i.e., whenever (Perceived Value – Actual Price) > 0].

### Adding a Behavioral Component

To complement this economic perspective, we now add a "behavioral" or "psychological" perspective to product pricing. This perspective captures "how fair a deal" one is getting. To make this point clear, consider the following scenarios first proposed by Professor Richard Thaler. [6]

*Scenario #1:*

*You are lying on the beach on a hot day. All you have to drink is ice water. For the past hour, you have been thinking about how much you would enjoy a nice cold bottle of your favorite beer. A friend gets up to make a phone call and offers to bring back a bottle of your favorite beer from the only nearby place where beer is sold — a small, run down-grocery store. He says that the beer might be expensive and asks how much you are willing to spend. He says he will not buy the beer if it costs more than the price you state. What price do you tell your friend?*

What is your "perceived value" for a nice cold bottle of your favorite beer brought to you on a hot beach? Once you have decided upon the price you would tell your friend, consider a second scenario, identical to the first, except for the source of the beer, which is underlined.

*Scenario #2:*

*You are lying on the beach on a hot day. All you have to drink is ice water. For the past hour, you have been thinking about how much you would enjoy a nice cold bottle of your favorite beer. A friend gets up to make a phone call and offers to bring back a bottle of your favorite beer from the only nearby place where beer is sold — a fancy resort hotel. He says that the beer might be expensive and asks how much you are willing to spend. He says he will not buy the beer if it costs more than the price you state. What price do you tell your friend?*

If you are like most people, your responses to these two scenarios differ. When Thaler presented these scenarios to a group of executives in the early 1980s, the median response in the grocery store scenario was $1.50 and the median response in the fancy resort hotel scenario was $2.65. Similar results repeatedly have been obtained using Harvard MBAs — albeit, with somewhat higher average prices.

---

6 Scenarios 1 and 2 have been adapted from Richard H. Thaler's paper, "Mental Accounting and Consumer Choice," *Marketing Science*, 4, 3 (Summer 1985): p. 199-214.

The interesting question is why? As pointed out by Thaler, for the person consuming the beer on the beach, nothing of importance has changed between the two scenarios. Specifically,

- in both scenarios, the ultimate consumption is identical — the same beer is consumed on the same beach.

- no atmosphere from the fancy resort hotel or the run-down grocery store is being consumed by the beer drinker to justify different prices.

- there is no strategic reason to report a price below one's "perceived value" for the beer [e.g., you cannot haggle over price with hotel or store owner].

As a result, a person's "perceived value" for the beer *should be* identical across the two scenarios. To report otherwise would suggest that a bottle of beer consumed on a beach somehow tastes better or quenches thirst more effectively when purchased from one location than another. In turn, if the "perceived value" of the beer should be identical across the two scenarios, a person's "willingness to pay" also should be identical across the two scenarios.

Yet people's prices do differ and it appears that this difference is due to *expectations* consumers have regarding the price of a bottle of beer at a fancy hotel versus a run-down grocery store. As noted by Thaler, "While paying $2.50 for a beer is an expected annoyance at the resort hotel, it would be considered an outrageous 'rip-off' in a grocery store."

In the end, it appears that one's "willingness to pay" in these two scenarios is driven not only by the "economic utility" of the transaction [i.e., perceived value – price], but also by the "psychological utility" of the transaction, driven largely by a consumer's perception of "fairness." Over the next several pages, we will look at scenarios that highlight specific drivers of transaction "fairness" and of the "psychological utility" of a transaction.

## Some Behavioral Updates to the Economic Perspective

### 1. The Relative versus Absolute Value of Money

In the economic approach to pricing, all money is equal – e.g., $10 in one transaction is worth the same as $10 in another transaction. Research suggests that this may not be the case when it comes to one's willingness to pay, however. Consider the following scenario and think about how you would respond.[7] There are no right or wrong answers. There is only your intuition as to how you would behave if you found yourself in such a scenario.

*Scenario #3:*

*You set off to buy a Sony Walkman at what you believe to be the cheapest store in the area. Upon arriving, you find that the Walkman you want costs $29, a price consistent with your prior expectations. As you are about to make the purchase, a reliable friend tells you that the very same Walkman is selling for $10 less at a store approximately 10 minutes away. Do you go to the other store to buy the Walkman?*

---

7 Scenarios 3 and 4 have been adapted from Richard H. Thaler's paper, "Toward a Positive Theory of Consumer Choice," *Journal of Economic Behavior and Organization*, 1 (1980), p. 39-60.

What would you do? Do you go to the other store and save $10 or do you simply go ahead and purchase the Walkman in the first store and pay $29?

A purely economic approach to this question would be to ask yourself whether 10 minutes of your time is worth $10. If you decide that 10 minutes of your time is more valuable than $10, you should forget about the potential savings and purchase the Walkman at the first store for $29. If, however, you decide that 10 minutes of your time is less valuable than $10, you should travel to the second store and purchase the desired Walkman there for $19.

Now consider a second scenario, identical to the first, except for the nature and the price of the product being purchased.

*Scenario #4:*

*You set off to buy a Sony Camcorder at what you believe to be the cheapest store in the area. Upon arriving, you find that the Camcorder you want costs $495, a price consistent with your prior expectations. As you are about to make the purchase, a reliable friend tells you that the very same Walkman is selling for $10 less at a store approximately 10 minutes away. Do you go to the other store to buy the Camcorder?*

From the economic perspective, if you decided to travel to the second store to save $10 in the first scenario, you also should have decided to travel to the second store to save $10 in this second scenario. In both scenarios, the tradeoff is $10 for 10 minutes of your time.

If you are like most people, however, your natural inclination will be to answer "yes" in Scenario #3 and "no" in Scenario #4. After all, $10 on a $29 Walkman represents a savings of over 33%, but $10 on a $495 Camcorder represents a savings of a measly 2%. While the dollar savings are the same, the psychological value of the savings is far greater in the first scenario than the second. Whereas a $10 savings on a $29 Walkman is perceived as a "fair" (and even generous) incentive to travel to the second store, a $10 savings on a $495 camcorder is perceived as a rather inadequate incentive to travel to the second store.

These two scenarios raise a curious and important fact about money. Namely, the "psychological utility" of a fixed amount of money (e.g., $10) is relative. Saving $10 on a $29 item will have much greater impact on a consumer's behavior than saving $10 on a $495 item.

This directly carries over to a consumer's willingness to pay. Imagine two consumers, one of whom is debating whether to pay $19 for a Walkman that he values at $29, the other of whom is debating whether to pay $485 for a camcorder that he values at $495. While both consumers have the same "economic utility" to enter their respective transactions [i.e., perceived value – price = $10 in both cases], the first consumer will be more likely to make a purchase than the second due to the higher relative incentive to enter his transaction.

This leads to our first update to the economic perspective:

**Behavioral Update #1: Willingness to Pay is Impacted by Relative Incentives**

In determining his willingness to pay, a consumer will consider both his absolute "economic utility" from the transaction [i.e., perceived value – actual price] and his relative incentive to enter the transaction [i.e., (perceived value – actual price)/(actual price)].

## 2. The Impact of a Salient Reference Price

Expectations about "what a product will cost" also seem to impact a consumer's "willingness to pay." [8] Read the following scenario and think about how you would respond. Again, there are no right or wrong answers. Only your intuition matters.

Scenario #5

*Your favorite sports team has made the playoffs. Its first-round playoff series is a best-of-seven series[9] with Games 1, 2, 5, and 7 played on your team's home field. General admission tickets had been priced at $20 during the regular season. The team decided to raise general admission prices to $40 for these four playoff games. Is this price increase fair or unfair?*

Is it fair for a sports team to raise prices by $20 between the regular season and the playoffs? Most people who encounter this scenario say "yes." About two-thirds of Harvard MBAs not only believe it to be "fair," but would expect such an increase. Arguments in support of this stance include:

- The nature of the product has changed – playoff games are more exciting than regular season games.
- Demand almost certainly will be higher for the playoff games and the team is merely responding to this increase in demand.
- It is common for ticket prices to increase for playoff games.

Now consider a second scenario, similar to the first scenario except for the timing of the $20 price increase.

Scenario #6

*Your favorite sports team has made the playoffs. Its first-round playoff series is a best-of-seven series with Games 1, 2, 5, and 7 played on your team's home field. General admission tickets had been priced at $20 during the regular season. General admission tickets were also priced at $20 for Games 1 and 2 of the playoffs. After Game 2, the team decided to raise prices to $40 for Games 5 and 7. Is this price increase fair or unfair?*

In considering this second scenario, note that from a purely economic perspective, if Games 5 and 7 are worth $40 in Scenario #5, they should also be worth $40 in Scenario #6. Therefore, any difference in "fairness" between the two scenarios is not being driven by a change in the "economic utility" of the transaction, as measured by [perceived value – price], but by the "psychological utility" of the transaction.

---

[8] In these and subsequent scenarios, individuals are being asked to assess the "fairness" of a firm's pricing decision. Perceptions of fairness should impact "willingness to pay" in a straightforward fashion. In particular, in the short-term, consumers will be less willing to pay a price they feel is "unfair." In the long-term, consumers will be less likely to purchase from a firm that makes an unfair pricing decision.

[9] In a best-of-seven series, the teams play games until one team wins four. This guarantees a minimum of four games and a maximum of seven. Often, Games 1, 2, 5, and 7 are played at one teams location, Games 3, 4 and 6 are played at the other teams location. Also, for each of Games 5, 6 and 7, tickets often are not sold until it is apparent that each game will be required.

If you are like most individuals, however, you find the price increase in Scenario #6 to be "unfair." What seems to drive this sense of unfairness is the fact that ticket prices were raised mid-playoffs. Once ticket prices were set for Games 1 and 2, those prices created an expectation for prices for the remainder of the playoffs. By raising prices for Games 5 and 7, this expectation was violated.

These two scenarios highlight the power of a salient "reference price," a price against which consumers compare other prices to assess both the "goodness" and "fairness" of a given transaction. In Scenario #5, regular season ticket prices were not a salient (nor appropriate) reference price due to the fundamental difference between regular season games and playoff games. In contrast, in Scenario #6, ticket prices for playoff Games 1 and 2 did establish a salient (and seemingly appropriate) reference price for Games 5 and 7. As a result, price changes in Scenario #5 are deemed "fair" while price changes in Scenario #6 are deemed "unfair."

Interestingly, Scenario #6 was actually played out in the spring of 1997. In a best-of-seven playoff series between basketball's Miami Heat and New York Knicks, Miami raised ticket prices in the middle of the playoff series. For Games 1 and 2, Miami Heat management had set the prices for various seats at $20, $30 and $40. After Game 2, the Heat raised ticket prices to $50, $80 and $90 for Game 5. Public outrage resulted and Game 5 was one of the very few basketball playoff games that year not to sell out. The extent of the outrage forced Miami Heat management to return prices to $20, $30 and $40 for the final and deciding Game 7.

In more mainstream consumer transactions, how are reference prices formed? The most common basis for a reference price is the previous price paid for a product. If a consumer has been paying $9.99 for bottle of wine that they have come to enjoy, this $9.99 price becomes this person's reference price for the wine. If the consumer subsequently encounters the same bottle of wine at the same store for $14.99, the price difference will likely be questioned — not because the wine isn't worth $14.99 to the consumer, but because the consumer has grown to view $9.99 as the "fair price." This concept is captured in our second update to the economic perspective:

**Behavioral Update #2: Willingness to Pay is Impacted by Salient Reference Prices**

In determining her willingness to pay, a consumer will consider her "economic utility" from the transaction [i.e., perceived value – actual price] and the consistency between the actual price and a salient reference price [i.e., actual price – reference price].

## 3. The Impact of a Firm's Cost of Goods Sold

Scenarios #5 and #6 show that a salient reference price can impact a consumer's perception of fairness (and, by extension, her willingness to pay). Another factor that impacts a consumer's perception of "fairness" is a firm's cost of goods sold, as indicated by the following two scenarios.[10]

Scenario #7:

*A grocery store has no peanut butter in stock, but is about to receive a new shipment. Prior to delivery, the owner finds out that the wholesale price of peanut butter has increased 20% and will affect this new shipment. The owner decides to increase the price of the new peanut butter by 20%. Is this retailer's actions fair or unfair?*

10 These two scenarios are adapted from Kahneman, Knetsch and Thaler, "Fairness as a Constraint on Profit Seeking: Entitlements in the Market," *American Economic Review 76*, 4 (1986): p. 728-741.

With little argument, most consumers find this retailer's actions to be entirely "fair." After all, the retailer is only passing along a wholesale price increase to the consumer. The retailer has not caused the price increase and is not benefiting from it. Contrast that with the following scenario:

Scenario #8:

*A grocery store has a one week supply of peanut butter in stock and is due to receive a new shipment in the near future. Prior to delivery, the owner finds out that the wholesale price of peanut butter has increased 20% and will affect the new shipment. The owner decides to immediately increase the shelf price on his current stock of peanut butter by 20%. Is this retailer's actions fair or unfair?*

In thinking about these two scenarios, let us again consider the purely economic perspective. In particular, one's "perceived value" for peanut butter should not differ between the two scenarios – the peanut butter is the same in both scenarios. In addition, the price being charged for the peanut butter has increased 20% in both cases. Therefore, any sense of "fairness" is not being driven by the "economic utility" of the transaction [i.e., perceived value – actual price], but by the "psychological utility" of the transaction.

Nonetheless, most consumers find the retailer's actions "unfair" in Scenario #8. Why? The typical argument is that this retailer is only entitled to pass on a cost increase on a product that has been subject to that increase. In Scenario #8, by raising the price of the in-stock peanut butter that has not been subject to the wholesale price increase, the retailer is "taking advantage of the consumer."

In addition to the magnitude of their own incentive to purchase, these two scenarios suggest that consumers are concerned with the magnitude of the firm's incentive to sell [i.e., actual price – cost of goods sold]. In particular, consumers do not want to be taken advantage of and desire a fair division of value between themselves and the firm that makes a product. As a result, they are willing to label a price increase "unfair" when that price increase is coupled with little or no change in the cost of goods sold. This concept is captured in our third update to the economic perspective.

**Behavioral Update #3: Willingness to Pay is Impacted by Cost of Goods Sold**

In determining his willingness to pay, a consumer will consider his own "economic utility" from the transaction [i.e., perceived value – actual price] and that of the firm [i.e., actual price – cost of goods sold].

## 4. The Nature of the Product Being Sold

To this point, it has been shown that factors such as a salient reference price or a known cost of goods sold can impact perceptions of transaction fairness. How do these perceptions of fairness vary by the type of product being sold? Consider the following scenario:

Scenario #9

*In 1996, baseball's Seattle Mariners made it to the American League playoffs. During the season, general admission to a Mariners game cost $15. For the playoffs, the Mariners raised the price of general admission tickets to $20. Is this fair or unfair?*

Most individuals who encounter this scenario feel that this price increase is fair and justified, for many of the same reasons that a ticket price increase in Scenario #5 was fair and justified. In particular, the underlying conditions have changed (playoffs vs. regular season) and consumer demand almost certainly will increase. Under those conditions, a price increase is reasonable and should be expected. Now contrast this first scenario with the following:

<u>*Scenario #10*</u>

*A hardware store had been selling snow shovels for $15. The morning after a large snowstorm, the store raises the price of its snow shovels to $20. Is this fair or unfair?* [11]

From an economic perspective, the arguments that support a price increase in Scenario #9 also seem to apply in Scenario #10. In this second scenario, the underlying conditions have changed (snow vs. no snow) and demand almost certainly will increase.

Nonetheless, while the price increase in the first scenario generally is viewed as "fair," the price increase in the second scenario is almost universally viewed as "unfair." Why the difference? One possible explanation lies in the nature of the product being promoted. Whereas the purchase of tickets to a Seattle Mariners playoff game is viewed as a discretionary expense, a purchase of a snow shovel after a large snowstorm is viewed as a necessary expense. As a result, to raise the price of tickets when your team makes it to the playoffs is viewed as legitimate, but to raise the price of snow shovels after a snowstorm is viewed as exploitation.

These final two scenarios provide our last update to the economic model.

**<u>Behavioral Update #4</u>: Perceptions of Fairness Vary Across Product Categories**

In determining her willingness to pay, the degree to which a consumer will rely upon her "economic utility" from the transaction [i.e., perceived value – actual price] will vary across product categories (e.g., discretionary vs. necessity, luxury vs. utilitarian).

## Managing Perceptions of Transaction Fairness

This note was designed to highlight some of the psychological drivers of consumer price response. As captured in **Figure B**, it adds a behavioral component to the more familiar economic approach to product pricing.

**Figure B** Combining the Economic and Behavioral Drivers of Willingness to Pay

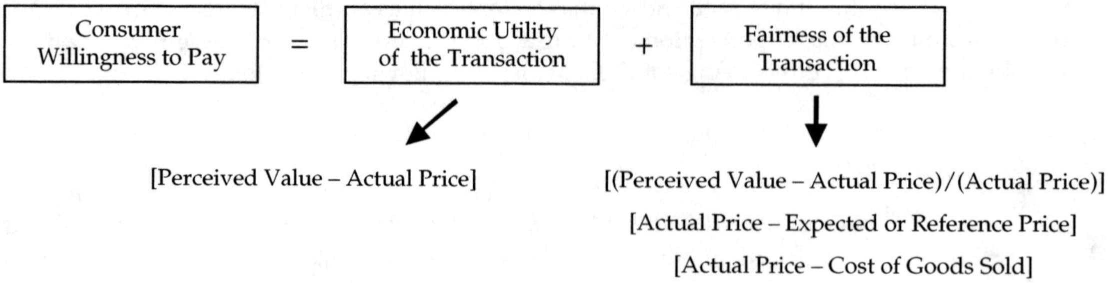


[11] Scenario #10 is adapted from Kahneman, Knetsch and Thaler, "Fairness as a Constraint on Profit Seeking: Entitlements in the Market," *American Economic Review 76*, 4 (1986): p. 728-741.

This framework suggests that an economically rational consumer *should* decide whether to buy a product solely on the economic utility of the transaction — i.e., by comparing perceived value to product price. In reality, consumers incorporate a host of psychological or behavioral factors into their decision making. These factors include the relative size of the incentive to purchase, the consistency between actual price and expected price, and the difference between product price and the firm's cost of goods sold. These behavioral factors influence perceptions of transaction "fairness" and tend to reduce a consumer's willingness to pay relative to a purely economic perspective.

Armed with these insights, however, how can a firm more effectively manage perceptions of transaction fairness and anticipate a consumer's willingness to pay for its products. Two strategies are recommended.

## Strategy #1: Actively Manage Price Expectations

A consumer usually enters a transaction with some expectation about the price of a product. As evidenced by the scenarios presented in this note, these expectations can have systematic and significant effects on that consumer's willingness to pay for the product. Unfortunately, firms often do very little to understand and/or manage these expectations.

Instead, firms should actively manage the reference prices and comparisons that consumers employ when assessing product prices. In particular, a firm should look to:

- **Establish credible reference prices.** A firm should look to establish a benchmark price for its products whenever possible. Common tools for doing this include the use of a credible "suggested retail price" or "list price." Through the clear posting and reliance upon list prices, the automobile industry has done a good job of managing the benchmark price against which consumers evaluate the fairness of the final price paid.

- **Manage product price trends.** The single most influential reference price that consumers employ when assessing the fairness of a product price it the previous price paid for that product. As a result, it is far easier to lower prices that are too high than to raise prices that are too low.

- **Encourage favorable comparisons.** Consumers naturally compare the prices of products within and across product categories. In anticipation of this reliance upon comparisons, a firm could suggest comparisons for consumers to consider. For instance, to combat the perception of excessively high prices for its cereals, Kellogg might be well-advised to compare the daily cost of its cereals (about 30¢) to the cost of other breakfast alternatives, such as the cost of a donut or bagel (50¢ or more).

- **Avoid unfavorable comparison through product differentiation.** When compact discs first appeared in the music market, they suffered from price comparisons to vinyl records. At $15, CDs were about twice the price of the alternative they were replacing. It was only after convincing consumers that such comparisons were inappropriate, due to vast improvements in sound quality and scratch resistance, that consumers accepted the higher CD prices as fair and reasonable.

## Strategy #2: Actively Manage Perceptions of Cost of Goods Sold

As Scenarios #7 and #8 suggest, consumers are sensitive to a firm's cost of goods sold. As a general rule, consumers are reluctant to pay for products they perceive to be overpriced relative to cost.

This consideration of COGS is especially problematic for firms that operate under high fixed and low variable costs. For example, Microsoft charges hundreds of dollars for its software, yet can churn out incremental copies of that software at the cost of a floppy disk. Many consumers view this as "unfair" and, as a result, have few qualms about using pirated software. In a similar vein, some consumer label drug companies as "greedy" when those companies charge $40 or $50 for a single dose of a branded drug when comparable generics cost a fraction of the price.

Such thinking on the part of the consumer fails to appreciate the fully-loaded cost of product delivery. In the case of Microsoft, the incremental cost of producing another copy of Windows pales in comparison to the cost of developing and supporting that application. And in the case of the drug company, many years and many millions of dollars may have gone into the research and development needed to bring that drug to market. These examples highlight the need for firms to manage the consumers' perceptions of cost of goods sold. This can be accomplished in several ways.

- **Focus attention of fully-loaded cost of goods sold.** For firms in high fixed cost/low variable cost industries, it is difficult to justify high product prices based on the incremental cost of production. Rather, the firm can focus consumer attention on the fully-loaded cost of production. For instance, if drug companies and software developers effectively communicated the high cost of product development and product support to consumers, they may successfully combat impressions of pricing "unfairly."

- **Bundle products to obscure cost of goods sold.** Some firms sell products where costs are readily apparent to the consumer (e.g., personal computer retailers). Other firms choose to bundle those very same products with additional goods or services so as to obscure the true cost of goods sold. For example, rather than sell computer components, value-added resellers sell turn-key systems. And rather than sell tickets to sporting events, travel agents sell vacation packages that include airfare, hotel and game tickets. By bundling products, a firm can make its costs less transparent to consumers.

- **Focus attention of consumer value.** A final means by which firms can look to minimize the impact of cost of goods sold is by focusing attention on the consumer's incentive to purchase. In the end, a consumer benefits whenever perceived value is greater than product price, regardless of the firm's cost of goods sold. As such, through effective product positioning and communication of value, a firm can minimize the impact of COGS by maximizing attention to the net benefit of purchase to the consumer.

## Summary

This note began with the statement, "It is important for a firm to get its pricing 'right.'" Yet, "getting prices right" is a complex process that few firms seem well-equipped to manage. While firms have a relatively good grasp of the readily available economic inputs to the pricing decision (e.g., cost of goods sold, price of substitutes), most lack the behavioral inputs needed to fully understand and anticipate a consumers response to a pricing change. In particular, few firms anticipate the behavioral implications of transaction "fairness," as perceived by the consumer. This note does not attempt to offer a comprehensive behavioral perspective to pricing. Rather, it is meant to raise awareness that behavioral factors exist and that these factors are important if a firm expects to "get its pricing right."

## ISSUES OF PRODUCT POLICY

(M. Sarvary / 9-500-027 / 10 pages)

### Summary

Explores the basic vocabulary and issues related to product policy within a firm.

### Outline

The Product Mix
Product Differentiation
Managing Products over Their Lifecycle

### Learning Objectives

### Questions and Exercises

1. In thinking about product policy, consider the relative roles of marketing vs. other business functions or departments in your company. Who, as a practical matter, has the greatest control over shaping and changing policy for major brands or lines? If your firm has classic product or brand managers, do they think of themselves as marketers? Is their background in marketing or some other functional area? Analyzing and understanding these matters might help you to recognize special skills and strengths you can contribute to product management.

2. How strong is your company at developing what the author calls "augmented products"? Gather with a group of your colleagues and evaluate a sampling of the firm's products. You might consider focusing on the concentric circles in Figure 1 to provide a visual aid as you consider what the company has added to its core products to augment value? Has your company taken advantage of this concept or is it still taking the "a wrench is just a wrench" approach?

# Issues of Product Policy

In some sense products "define" the firm in the eyes of the consumer. An important difference between product policy and other marketing mix variables is that product decisions are relatively hard to change. As such, they require a much more forward-looking perspective.

Throughout this note, the word *product* is used in a broad sense and really should be thought of as a bundle of customer benefits. This definition may include physical products but often it also includes packaging and the services offered with the product. The entire package is often referred to as the augmented product. Sometimes the product is nothing but a service (e.g. consulting services, passenger airlines, etc.).

This note has three sections. First, we discuss the notion and characteristics of a "product mix". The second part addresses the problem of product differentiation. The last section discusses issues that are related to the product's lifecycle.

## 1. The Product Mix

Most companies are multi-product organizations, often producing a variety of different product lines. L'Oréal for example, offers a number of different products under the Plénitude brand name. Individual **products** have separate designations on the seller's list and include different flavors, colors, forms or sizes. A **product line** is a group of related products satisfying a particular class of needs or being used together. They usually possess common characteristics, are sold through the same distribution channels and fall within the same price range. The **product mix** is all the products offered by the firm. Not every product or even product line needs to be profitable within the product mix. However, the product mix as a whole should be *the* optimal mix to ensure the overall profitability of the firm. As such, certain products may only contribute to profitability by complementing others. For example, products might be carried only to appeal to customers who want to deal with a full-line supplier.

Since elements of the product mix generally exhibit some form of synergy, product decisions affect individual products, product lines or the entire product mix of the firm. Three general concepts are important to characterize the product mix: breadth, depth and consistency. **Breadth** refers to the number of product lines carried by the firm. **Depth** designates the average number of items (e.g. sizes, colors, weights) offered in each product line. **Consistency** of product mix alludes to the degree

*Professor Miklos Sarvary prepared this note as the basis for class discussion rather than to illustrate either effective or ineffective handling of an administrative situation. Professor John Deighton provided part of the material.*

of similarity between product lines in end use, technology and production techniques, distribution channels etc.

Depending on two factors, corporate objectives and company resources, firms may pursue different strategies when designing their product mix. The two extremes are (i) follow a policy of **diversity** and (ii) concentrate efforts to a narrow product mix. In the former case the product mix has great breadth and depth and may have less consistency across products (for example GE). In the latter case the firm offers a few closely related or similar products (e.g. Swatch). L'Oréal's Plénitude brand falls somewhere between the two extreme cases. Each of the extremes has advantages and disadvantages. A policy of diversity may ensure higher stability in overall demand for the firm. However, it may require more careful logistics and coordination on the production side. Also, it might dilute the overall image of the firm. In contrast, a highly focused product mix may present less challenge in logistics but may be more risky and requires more careful demand analysis (e.g. to avoid cannibalization between similar products).

## 2. Product Differentiation

Product differentiation is an important part of product positioning. As we have seen, one role of the positioning statement is to clearly articulate to consumers the benefits that the product fulfills. However, the firm does not want to introduce products targeted at needs that are already served by competitors. In such situations consumers simply choose the cheaper firm and competitors have an incentive to undercut each other's price. This leads to intense price competition and leaves no profit to the firm. To avoid price competition the product needs to be clearly **differentiated** from other offerings. Both L'Oréal and Becton Dickinson face the problem of how to differentiate their offerings from that of competition in relatively mature product categories. We distinguish two types of differentiation labeled **horizontal** and **vertical,** respectively.

### Horizontal Differentiation:

Horizontal differentiation is a positioning strategy that makes use of the fact that consumers differ in their *tastes*. In the category of passenger cars for example, some consumers like small cars, others like big trucks while still others like sport cars. Each of these groups consists of a relatively homogeneous set of people with similar needs. The idea of horizontal differentiation is to identify the group(s) whose need(s) are not served by a competitor.

The standard tool to identify possible un-served needs is the perceptual map. It is relatively easy to spot on the map empty areas, i.e. a combination of attributes not covered by products. These represent opportunities for new, differentiated product introductions. It is not clear however, that these opportunities should be explored. The attribute combinations in question may not be technically feasible (supply-side constraint). Alternatively, the identified area may represent an insufficient number of consumers (demand-side constraint). The goal is to select un-served needs that can be profitably realized.

### Vertical Differentiation:

Vertical differentiation also exploits the fact that consumers are different. However, it takes advantage of a different source of consumer heterogeneity, namely that consumers differ in their *willingness to pay for quality*. In a pure vertical differentiation problem, consumers agree on a unique relevant dimension driving their preferences. We call this dimension "quality". Quality may be the combination (e.g. the weighted average) of many complementary attributes. In the case of passenger cars for example, it can be a combination of speed, comfort and reliability. All consumers agree that these are the relevant dimensions contributing to quality and they all prefer more quality to less. They only differ in their valuation of quality. Staying with the example of passenger cars, most consumers prefer a BMW to a Ford, but few can (or would be willing to) pay the price for the BMW. Vertical differentiation amounts to positioning products to consumers with a specific willingness to pay for quality un-served by a competitor.

Perceptual maps can also provide guidance for vertical differentiation. In product categories where preferences are taste driven, perceptual maps exhibit "ideal points" representing segments of consumers with distinct tastes. In product categories where quality is the key determinant of preferences, the perceptual map often produces an "ideal direction", which essentially represents consumers' perception of quality. Successful products tend to line up along this direction. Which attributes and to what extent contribute to the perception of quality is itself an important question for the marketer. Also, it is easy to spot empty segments on the quality dimension indicating possible opportunities for the introduction of new products.

## Horizontal and Vertical Differentiation in Practice:

In most product categories, marketers have the option to differentiate their products both along quality as well as in terms of customer tastes (think of perfumes for example, or L'Oréal's Plénitude line). Creativity plays an important role in this task. New product dimensions can be discovered that are important to segments, which have not been thought of by consumers before (think of IBM taken by surprise with the emergence of the PC category). The firm can sometimes change the entire paradigm of differentiation. Product categories where preferences are largely performance driven may be differentiated horizontally (think of Apple's iMac or Swatch's redefinition of the watches category).

The primary time for thinking about differentiation is in the phase of product concept development. The firm should strive to develop products that are differentiated from competitors'. However, other elements of the marketing mix also have an important role in differentiation. Advertising is an obvious tool to communicate to consumers to what extent and along what dimensions is the product different from other alternatives. Price can be an important signal of quality and thus it is a tool for vertical differentiation. Packaging can be key for differentiation (think of the importance of packaging for "green" consumers, for example).

One of the most important tools of differentiation is customer service. As products mature, all competitors can efficiently deliver the same core product attributes. Then, the only way to create a sustainable differentiated offering is through special customer services. This leads to, what we call the *augmented* product (see figure 1). Car dealerships for example, offer roughly the same core products (similar selection of cars) but they differentiate themselves on the type and amount of services that they offer to customers. Services are an efficient tool for differentiation because they are relatively hard to copy by competitors compared to other marketing mix elements. In contrast to physical products, it is hard to quantify the additional profit generated by services. However, it is relatively easy to see the extra expenditures that they represent. Because to most firms, services appear to be a risky investment, competitors are reluctant to match services in the short run.

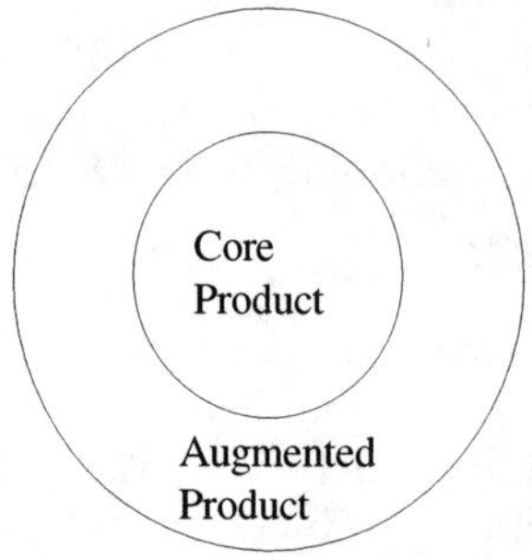


Figure 1: The augmented product[1]

## The Role of Brands in Product Differentiation:

It helps to start to think about brands simply as nouns that marketers have introduced into consumers' language to make product differentiation concrete. At a minimum, we want to assert that our offering is not like our competitors' offerings. When we call something Snapple, we are asserting that it is worth noting some special distinctions between Snapple and all other fruit juices. Some of these assertions can be viewed as promises or pledges about attributes of the product that cannot be verified before buying. Other assertions may have to do with how Snapple users are differentiated from Cola users, or how Snapple usage occasions are differentiated from other beverage usage occasions. Most ambitiously, a brand can assert that it *is* the category. Perhaps the highest goal to which a brand builder can aspire is to have the noun that he/she has imposed on the language displace the natural language word. For example, facial tissue was displaced by Kleenex, acetaminophen became Tylenol, online book buying became Amazon and we speak of Fedexing a package or Xeroxing a document.

Rich meanings accumulate around brands, as they do around all the nouns in language. Some of these meanings derive from the marketer's assertions, pledges and promises, but not all. Brands come to mean things the marketer may not have intended, as for example when Perrier came to mean 'polluted with benzene.' It is often the case that consumers co-create the meanings of brands, taking the marketer's efforts and turning them to their own purposes, as for example motorcycle gangs did with Harley Davidson. Building a brand is a complex meaning-making negotiation. It takes time, costs money, and often fails. But if it succeeds, the sum of the meanings attached to the brand constitutes an asset, called brand equity that may be among the corporation's most valuable properties.

Brands, like all nouns, *denote* and *connote*. That is, they point to things (denotation) and convey the significations of those things (connotation). To a builder of brands, it is important to note that unless the brand is useful for denoting, it will not survive long enough to connote anything.

How can we ensure that a brand denotes something useful? It may help to think of the consumer as navigating an unfamiliar landscape, and turning to the brand as a navigation aid or signpost. We do not want to create more signposts than the customer needs, and certainly not fewer. As an illustration, you may find that your credit card carries as many as three brands. It may bear a bank or affinity group's brand, an issuer like First USA or Associates, and a network like Cirrus or Plus. These are all attempts at service differentiation through brand building. Will they all succeed? Do consumers care for so many signposts? If you need to draw cash in a distant city, you may need

[1] Theodore Levitt (1980), "Marketing Success Through Differentiation - of Anything", *Harvard Business Review*, (February).

the Cirrus brand. If you want to avoid intrusive telemarketing from an aggressive card issuer, you may need the issuer's brand. In all likelihood, every experience differentiating this card from the others in your wallet will, however, accrue to only the dominant brand. Many financial service brands struggle to denote anything that the consumer finds worthy of notice.

When you have solved the denoting problem, you can confront the connoting problem. A brand's connotations are, in effect, its *reputation*. And like all reputations, they are partly the result of being inherently good or bad, and partly a matter of grandstanding. In a perfect world, a strong brand would be simply the reward for being a good product. However there is a great deal of stage management in brand building. We shall pick up that discussion in the note on integrated marketing communication.

## 3. Managing Products over Their Lifecycle

Innovations, including new products and brands go through what marketers call the product or brand "lifecycle". The lifecycle can be represented as a roughly bell-shaped curve, where the horizontal axis is time and the vertical axis is per period sales. While the actual shape (length, height, etc.) of the curve shows a lot of variation across products its general character is more or less identical. Figure 2 illustrates a typical product lifecycle. One can distinguish four typical phases of the lifecycle: (i) introduction, (ii) growth, (iii) maturity and (iv) decline.

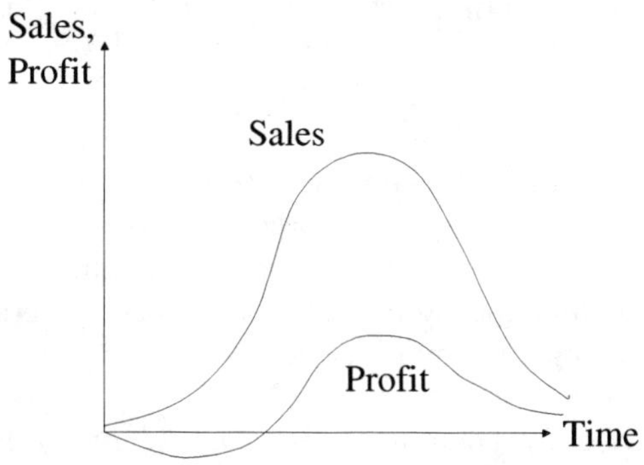


Figure 2: The product lifecycle.

In the **introduction** phase the firm typically invests in developing the market for the product (e.g. educating customers and finding appropriate distribution channels). Sales grow moderately and profits are typically negative. Rogers Communications, being the first company to sell high speed Internet access over its cable lines faces this type of environment. In the **growth** phase, the core problem of the firm is to gain market share and develop various forms of customer loyalty (e.g. develop a strong brand name). It also has to respond to increased competition attracted by its product's success. The **maturity** phase is generally characterized by a "shake-out" in the corresponding product category. Firms typically try to focus on locking up resources (e.g. distribution networks) and differentiating themselves from other players. Becton Dickinson faces this environment in the venous blood collection category. Finally, in the **decline** phase, there are only a few large firms, whose focus is on efficiency in a market where prices are low.

## The Product Diffusion Process

Why do products undergo a lifecycle? What is the social process underlying it? The product lifecycle can be nicely described with the following simple model, which is sometimes used by market researchers to forecast future demand:[2]

$$\text{Sales}_t = (a + b\frac{B_t}{M})(M - B_t)\,.$$

*M* represents the product's market potential (all the consumers who can potentially adopt it) and $B_t$ is the total number of customers who adopted it till today (*t*). This simple equation has two components, which represent two counteracting forces. The second says that, as the number of cumulative adopters (*B*) increases, sales will linearly decrease because the untapped market becomes smaller. The first part says that sales grow linearly with the number of cumulative adopters. This sales growth comes from two sources. First, it comes from a constant term, *a*, which represents consumers who make up their mind independently from others when they buy the product. They are called "innovators" by Rogers[3] and *a* is referred to as the "coefficient of innovation". The second term represents the "influence" of current customers on potential new ones; a phenomenon often called "word of mouth communication". The effect of this term is higher, as the firm's current customer base, *B* increases over time. The parameter *b* is called the "coefficient of imitation" and it measures the importance or effectiveness of word of mouth in the consumer population.

Understanding the product diffusion process is important for many reasons. The most important applications are (i) sales forecasting and (ii) marketing resource allocation.

### Sales Forecasting

Forecasting is typically used to calculate the optimal funding needed for the product launch or to plan production capacity. A business plan always exhibits a stream of forecasted sales figures. Finally, firms sequentially introduce new product generations. Intel, for example, introduces a new chip roughly every two years. Understanding the diffusion process is critical to avoid cannibalization and to efficiently migrate the existing customer base to the new product generation of the firm.

Forecasts can be obtained by generating the parameters of the model (market potential, coefficients of imitation and innovation) from the history of similar categories. For entirely new products without any sales history, this may be the only method available. If early sales data are available, then one can use statistical methods to estimate the diffusion curve. Such studies can be ordered from market research firms.

### Allocating Marketing Resources over Time

The diffusion model also provides guidelines on how to set marketing resources over the product lifecycle. For example, if the coefficient of imitation, *b* is large (i.e. there is strong word of mouth) then this calls for a "penetration pricing" strategy, where the firm prices low in the early stage to build a critical customer base. It also suggests that, in the early phase (when *B* is small), the target segment should be the people who tend to make up their mind independently from others (i.e. the innovators), because they are more likely to buy into the new product concept.

---

[2] Bass, Frank M. (1969), "A New Product Growth Model for Consumer Durables," *Management Science*, 15, 5, 215-227.

[3] Everett M. Rogers, The Diffusion of Innovations, New York: The Free Press 1983.

Research by Rogers found that people differ in their propensity to innovate. At the one extreme are the "innovators" who want to be the first to try everything. At the other extreme are the so-called "laggards" who are the very last to adopt a new concept. The majority of people lie along a continuum between these two extremes. As we move along the continuum, people's typical psychological and demographic profile changes quite systematically. Innovators tend to be younger, educated and mobile. They are more likely to take risks and they are venturesome. This pattern of consumer characteristics can help identifying early and late adopters for targeting purposes.

## New Product Success and Failure

In his best-selling books, Geoffrey Moore[4] uses the product diffusion paradigm to understand which products turn into success stories and why? He finds that there is a crucial distinction between the early adopters and a larger segment of the population that adopts right after them (called the "early majority" by Rogers): it is the distinction between marketing to visionaries and pragmatists.

| **Visionaries** | **Pragmatists** |
|---|---|
| Intuitive | Analytic |
| Support revolution | Support evolution |
| Break away from the pack | Stay with the herd |
| Contrarian | Conformist |
| Follow their own dictates | Consult with their colleagues |
| Take risks | Manage risks |
| Motivated by future opportunities | Motivated by present problems |
| Seek what is possible | Pursue what is probable |

In Moore's terms, most high technology companies face an **early market** populated by visionaries, and a **mainstream market** populated by pragmatists. He uses the phrase "crossing the chasm" to describe moving from the easy game, selling to visionaries in the early market, to the more difficult game, selling to pragmatists in the mainstream market, to emphasize the radical shift in marketing techniques needed to make this transition.

Moore uses the analogy of a bowling alley to describe how to "jump the chasm" and secure a foothold in the mainstream market. He argues that in the early stages, the mainstream market can be seen as a set of niche markets, arrayed like bowling pins, so that success in one niche can be transferred to an adjacent niche just as a strike on one bowling pin causes adjacent pins to fall.

A niche market on the mainstream side of the chasm is a small group of customers, all pragmatists, with closely related needs. They see the shape of the new paradigm, but they see plenty of life in the old paradigm. To entice them to adopt, the marketer must design a "whole product" for their niche, with none of the compromises that visionaries are willing to accept. Thereafter, the goal

[4] Geoffrey A. Moore, Inside the Tornado, New York: Harper Collins, 1995. Geoffrey A. Moore, Crossing the Chasm, New York: Harper Business, 1999.

is to replicate the plan in as many niches as possible until the product emerges as a leading standard across the broad mass of mainstream markets.

In Moore's terms, the 'bowling alley' phase of hi-tech market evolution is followed by the 'tornado' phase, so called because, with base infrastructure deployed and industry standards now visible to even the late majority, rapid and broad adoption of the winning standard occurs. This phase places tremendous demands on the ramp-up capability of those organizations that have managed the diffusion of innovation successfully to this point.

## How Innovative is the Product?

So far we have looked at how consumers and their interaction through word of mouth leads to the diffusion of a product. It is also useful to examine how the product itself may influence its acceptance by the customer base. One dimension to examine is: "to what extent will the product change the consumer's behavior?" Newness is for the consumer to decide. An innovation is a product or service whose adoption entails the disruption of established patterns of consumption: the more disruption, the more the product or service must be treated as innovative. Thus from a marketing perspective the question of whether something is new is for the consumer to make, not the developer of the technology.

Robertson[5] defines a **discontinuous innovation** as one that creates whole new patterns of consumption. Some discontinuous innovations make other patterns of consumption obsolete. Examples are PC-based word processing, which displaced the typewriter and e-mail, which displaced the fax, telegram and telex. Others do not displace an established technology, but change the way it is used. For example, the VCR led consumers to use television in different ways, and automatic teller machines changed the frequency with which human tellers were visited. Often more than one consumption system is affected, as for example when a consumer abandons supermarkets in favor of a home-delivered grocery service and, as a direct or indirect consequence, sells a minivan and buys a roadster. **Continuous innovations** are those which do not disrupt patterns of consumption, but are accommodated to smoothly. The introduction of tartar control toothpaste entailed little disruption, and was in this sense a continuous innovation. That kind of introduction is not the focus of this note.

Christensen[6] makes a subtly different distinction. He identifies two kinds of innovative technology or product: **sustaining and disruptive**. A sustaining innovation is one that improves on the performance of established products. A disruptive product under-performs established products in the near term, yet has enough appeal to find a niche among fringe segments or segments willing to take the long view. That niche grows until the mainstream market tips in its favor. In that way, niches can incubate the technologies that the mainstream buyer discovers suddenly to be discontinuous innovations. Examples are the personal computer, which under-performed the minicomputer at the time of its introduction, and thin film technology in hard disk construction.

---

[5] This section draws from Thomas S. Robertson, Innovative Behavior and Communication, New York: Holt, Reinhart & Winston, 1971, and from Hubert Gatignon and Thomas S. Robertson, "Innovative Decision Making" in Thomas S. Robertson and Harold H. Kassarjian, Handbook of Consumer Behavior, Engelwood Cliffs, N.J. 1991.

[6] Clayton Christensen, The Innovator's Dilemma: When New Technologies Cause Great Firms to Fail, Boston: Harvard Business School Press 1997.

## The Effect of Product Characteristics on Diffusion

Rogers identified six general attributes of an innovation that, he suggests, influence the speed and success of adoption. Later these have been arranged around the ACCORD acronym.[7]

- **(Relative) Advantage** - the degree to which the innovation is seen as superior to alternatives that it is intended to displace.
- **Compatibility** - the degree to which it is presented as consistent with the values and experiences of the consumer (the degree to which it is sustaining).
- **Complexity** - the degree to which it is easy to understand and use.
- **Observability** - the degree to which the results of adoption are observable and describable to others.
- **Riskiness** - the degree to which negative economic, social, or physical consequences can be foreseen.
- **Divisibility** - the degree to which it may be adopted gradually or tried on a limited basis.

Each of these attributes can be altered to some extent by choices in the marketing mix. They may be taken into account when developing the product itself. However, they may also be useful in identifying gaps and correcting them through other elements of the marketing mix. For example, relative advantage is affected directly by price. Complexity and observability may be affected by education through the communications campaign (e.g. product demonstrations, informative advertising, etc.). Observability, for example was an impediment to the diffusion of dish washing machines, until in-store demonstration overcame skepticism. Divisibility may be altered by free trials or rental programs. Before product launch, it is generally useful to collect information on how consumers perceive the new product on the ACCORD dimensions and adjust the marketing mix if necessary. Such information can be easily collected through focus groups or consumer surveys.

## New Product Development Process

New products are crucial to the health of firms, with some firms aiming to achieve 50% of sales from products no older than 5 years. In supermarkets alone, 16,000 products are introduced each year, of which between 80% and 90% fail to achieve a sustainable share of market and are withdrawn within two years. The cost of launching a new entrant into a major supermarket category such as detergents or prepared meals frequently exceeds $100 million. For most firms, new product development is a critical process. Typically, it is composed of the following stages:

- Idea generation
- Concept screening
- Business analysis

[7] Angelmar, Reinhard (1990), "Product innovation: A tool for competitive advantage", *European Journal of Operations Research*, 47, 182-189.

- Prototype development
- Test marketing
- Commercialization

Each step can be thought of as a filter that generates information to management about the likely success of the product. Only the most promising ideas make it through the filter, this way substantially reducing the cost of experimentation to the firm. As products move along the process, the higher the cost of experimentation. For example, test marketing is orders of magnitude more expensive (in the range of millions of dollars) than idea generation or concept screening (few thousand dollars). For the forward-looking firm, it is key to have an efficient product development process. Designing such a process should be part of the firm's dynamic marketing strategy.

## TORMENT YOUR CUSTOMERS (THEY'LL LOVE IT)

(S. Brown / #r0109e / 7p)

### Summary

This *Harvard Business Review* article makes a case for stepping away from "customer-centricity" and instead building customer desire and the perception of value by applying five provocative "retromarketing" principles: Make your product seem exclusive; shroud product developments in secrecy; amplify the product story, generating "buzz"; entertain your customers; be a trickster and tease your customers.

### Outline

Retro Shock
Going Retro
From Four P's to Pure Tease

### Learning Objectives

- Explore an alternative to the recent emphasis on customer focus and customer care.
- Understand the five key principles of retromarketing and tactics for applying them in the marketplace.

### Questions, Ideas, and Exercises

1. The author uses the following list of products and brands to exemplify at least one principle of retromarketing:

   Miata, Harley, Honda's Odyssey, and Chrysler's PT Cruiser
   De Beers diamonds
   Disney videos
   Ty Beanie Babies
   Scholastic's Harry Potter books
   Coke, Heinz Ketchup, Kentucky Fried Chicken, and Mrs. Fields' Cookies
   Calvin Klein
   Benetton
   Citroen
   Pizza Hut
   The movies *Planet of the Apes*, *Swordfish*, *AI*, and *Blair Witch Project*
   Tango fruit juice soda

   Can you perceive a common characteristic in these products? Could you use the author's principles to retromarket a purely utilitarian product? Or a product that is not truly distinctive in its marketplace? How well would the author's "play hard to get" approach work in your industry?

2. Consider this statement from the author: "The truth is, customers don't know what they want. They never have. They never will." While this may be a bold statement with regard to marketing, it is even bolder as a principle of new product development. To what extent is your company or industry "customer-centric" in developing products? Do you think this had led to your developing "me-too products," as the author says? Is there room in your industry or company culture for innovating by your own inspiration?

# Torment Your Customers (They'll Love It)

by Stephen Brown

Don't get me wrong: I have nothing against customers. Some of my best friends are customers. Customers are a good thing, by and large, provided they're kept well downwind.

My problem is with the concept of – and I shudder to write the term – "customer centricity." Everyone in business today seems to take it as a God-given truth that companies were put on this earth for one purpose alone: to pander to customers. Marketers spend all their time slavishly tracking the needs of buyers, then meticulously crafting products and pitches to satisfy them. If corporate functions were Dickens characters, marketing would be Uriah Heep: unctuous, ubiquitous, unbearable.

My friends, it's gone too far.

The truth is, customers don't know what they want. They never have. They never will. The wretches don't even know what they *don't* want, as the success of countless rejected-by-focus-groups products, from the Chrysler minivan to the Sony Walkman, readily attests. A mindless devotion to customers means me-too products, copycat advertising campaigns, and marketplace stagnation.

And customers don't really want to be catered to, anyway. I've spent most of my career studying marketing campaigns, and my research shows that many of the marketing coups of recent years have been far from customer centric. Or at least, the successes have proceeded from a deeper understanding of what people want than would ever emerge from the bowels of a data mine. Whatever people may desire of their products and services, they adamantly do not want kowtowing from the companies that market to them. They do not want us to prostrate ourselves in front of them and promise to love them, till death us do part. They'd much rather be teased, tantalized, and tormented by deliciously insatiable desire.

It's time to get back to an earlier marketing era, to the time when marketers ruled the world with creativity and style. It's time to break out the snake oil again. It's time for retromarketing.

> Retromarketing eschews the modern marketing proposition by deliberately holding back supplies. You want it? Can't have it. Try again later, pal.

## Retro Shock

Retromarketing is based on an eternal truth: Marketers, like maidens, get more by playing hard to get. That's the antithesis of what passes for modern marketing. These days, marketers aim to make life simple for the consumer by getting goods to market in a timely and efficient manner, so that they are available when and where they're wanted, at a price people are prepared to pay. Could anything be more boring? By contrast, retromarketing makes 'em work for it, by limiting availability, by delaying gratification, by heightening expectations, by fostering an enigmatic air of unattainability. It doesn't serve demand; it creates it.

As marketing strategies go, "Don't call us, we'll call you" is about as far from today's customer-hugging norm as it is possible to imagine. But it suits the times. We are, after all, in the midst of a full-blown nostalgia boom, a fact not lost on most successful product designers and advertisers. Retro is everywhere, whether it be Camel Lite's series of pseudonostalgic posters (a leather-helmeted flying ace lights up with a Zippo); Keds's television commercial for its old-style sneakers (reengineered, naturally, for today's demanding consumers); the McDonald's rollout of retrofitted diners (which offer table service and 1950s favorites like mashed potatoes and gravy); Disney's Celebration, a new olde town in Florida, just like the ones that never existed (outside of Hollywood studio back lots); or Restoration Hardware, a nationwide retail chain selling updated replicas of old-fashioned fixtures, fittings, and furnishings (perfect for redecorating that Rockwellian colonial in Celebration). Retro chic is de rigueur in everything from cameras, coffeepots, and radios to toasters, telephones, and refrigerators. Retro roller coasters, steam trains, airships, motorbikes, and ballparks are proliferating, as are reproductions of sports equipment from earlier days. Tiki bars are back; polyester jumpsuits are cavorting on the catwalks; shag carpet is getting laid in the most tasteful abodes; and retro autos, such as the PT Cruiser and the new T-Bird, are turning heads all around the country. It's reached the point, comedian George Carlin says, where we don't experience déjà vu, but vujà dé – those rare moments when we have an uncanny sense that what we're experiencing has *never happened before.*

People aren't just suckers for old-fashioned goods and services, they also yearn for the marketing of times gone by. They actually miss the days when a transaction was just a transaction, when purchasing a bar of soap didn't mean entering into a lifetime value relationship. Wary of CRM-inspired tactics, which are tantamount to stalking, they appreciate the true transparency of a blatant huckster. Retromarketing recognizes that today's consumer is nothing if not marketing savvy. Call it postmodern, but people enjoy the ironic art of a well-crafted sales pitch. The best of retromarketing hits consumers with the hardest of sells, all the while letting them in on the joke.

## Going Retro

Just like retrostyling, retromarketing is more art than science. It's easy to hit a false note. But can its lessons be spelled out? Is there an ABC for wannabes? They can, and there is. And although arrogant academicians always advocate acronyms, aphorisms, apothegms, and absurdly affected alliterations – to ensure ever-busy executives *get it* – retromarketing represents a rare renunciation of this ridiculous rhetorical rule. There are just five basic principles.

The first is that customers crave *exclusivity.* Retromarketing eschews the "here it is, come and get it, there's

***Stephen Brown*** *is a professor of marketing research at the University of Ulster in Northern Ireland and a visiting professor of marketing at Northwestern University's Kellogg School of Management in Evanston, Illinois. He has written 12 books on marketing, the latest of which is* Marketing: The Retro Revolution *(Sage, 2001).*

plenty for everyone" proposition – the modern marketing proposition – by deliberately holding back supplies and delaying gratification. You want it? Can't have it. Try again later, pal.

Granted, "Get it now while supplies last" is one of the oldest arrows in the marketing quiver. But it is no less effective for all that. First, exclusivity helps you avoid excess inventory – you don't make it until the customer begs for it. Second, it allows buyers to luxuriate in the belief that they are the lucky ones, the select few, the discerning elite. Promoting exclusivity is standard practice in the motor industry, as would-be buyers of Miatas, Harleys, and Honda Odysseys will readily testify. It's employed by De Beers for diamonds and Disney for videos. It's used by everyone from Wall Street brokers, with an IPO to pass off, to the chocolate conspirators at Cadbury, whose creme eggs are strictly rationed and highly seasonal. Indeed, it has launched countless one-day, 13-hour, blue-light, everything-must-go sales in retail stores the world over, and doubtless it will continue to do so.

Ty Warner, impresario of toy maker Ty Incorporated, may well go down in history for his ceaselessly inventive exploitation of exclusivity. To be sure, his velveteen storm troopers – the famous Beanie Babies – looked like undernourished attendees at the teddy bears' picnic. Nevertheless, their retromarketing campaign put Sun Tzu's *The Art of War* to shame. By coupling limited production runs with ruthless "retirements," Warner ensured that Beanie Babies remained in enormous demand and fostered a now-or-never mind-set among consumers and retailers.

Ostensibly priced at five or six bucks apiece, Beanies fetched upwards of three grand at auction and were known to trigger fistfights among frenzied I-spotted-it-first fans. They were sold through a plethora of small-time gift shops, bypassing major retail chains, whose EDI-driven ethos of regular supplies, no surprises, and guaranteed delivery times was anathema to Warner. Consistently inconsistent, he supplied what he wanted, when he wanted, to whomsoever he wanted, and if the retailers didn't like it, then they simply did without. When added to the constant introductions and retirements of models, the upshot was that Warner's wares were scattered hither and yon. Reason didn't enter into it, let alone rhyme. The tush-tagged creatures could thus be discovered in the most out-of-the-way outlets, which added to rather than detracted from Beanies' pseudonostalgic appeal. Fuelled, furthermore, by a massive word-of-mouse rumor mill, as well as an enormous secondary market in collectibles, Ty Warner turned the ultimate trick of making brand-new, mass-produced toys into semiprecious "antiques."

"Expect the unexpected" was Ty's rallying cry, and most would agree that capricious production, idiosyncratic distribution, eccentric promotion, and haphazard pricing are somewhat unusual in a modern marketing world of Analysis, Planning, Implementation, and Control. However, it is very much in keeping with a premodern milieu of restricted supply, excess demand, and multifarious channels of distribution. As Warner sagely observed, "As long as kids keep fighting over the products and retailers are angry at us because they cannot get enough, I think those are good signs." Indeed, the fighting would have continued had Warner not ultimately betrayed his own best retromarketing instincts. After deciding to terminate Beanie Babies en masse in December 1999, he was persuaded by an on-line plebiscite to grant a soft-toy stay of execution. Collectors were not amused, and Warner's iconic standing suffered irreparable damage.

Happily, right on Ty's heels came another tour de force of customer torment from the master marketers behind today's greatest mania: Harry Potter. Not only is J.K. Rowling's remarkable creation the perfect retro product – a twenty-first-century Tom Brown – but the wonderful wizard of Hogwarts has been marketed in an unashamedly retro manner. Scholastic's campaign for the blockbuster *Harry Potter and the Goblet of Fire* is a sterling example of the second principle of retromarketing: *secrecy.* It consisted of a complete blackout on advance information. The book's title, pagination, and price were kept under wraps until two weeks before publication. Review copies were withheld, no author interviews were allowed, and foreign translations were deferred for fear of injudicious leaks. Juicy plot details, including the death of a key character and Harry's sexual awakening, were drip fed to a slavering press corps prior to the launch. Printers and distributors were required to sign strict confidentially agreements. Booksellers were bound by a ruthlessly policed embargo, though some were allowed to display the tantalizing volume in locked cages for a brief period just before "Harry Potter Day," July 8, 2000. And in a stroke of retro genius, several advance copies were "accidentally" sold from an unnamed Wal-Mart in deepest West Virginia, though one of the "lucky" children was miraculously tracked down by the world's press and splashed across every front page worth its salt.

More sadistic still, Scholastic dropped less-than-subtle hints that there weren't enough copies of the book to go around, thereby exacerbating the gotta-get-it frenzy of fans and distributors alike. In the event, the tome was ubiquitously unavoidable, available everywhere from grocery stores to roadside restaurants. No one complained, of course, because everyone had managed to get their hands on the precious Potter, and by the time they'd finished reading the magical mystery, they'd forgotten its magically mysterious marketing campaign. Now you see it, now you don't.

Whereas modern marketing is upfront, above board, and transparent, retro revels in mystery, intrigue, and covert operations. Consider the classic "secret" recipes that have helped to purvey all sorts of comestibles – Coca-Cola, Heinz Ketchup, Kentucky Fried Chicken, Mrs. Fields Cookies, the list goes on – to say nothing of cosmetics (the secret of youthfulness), proprietary medicines (the secret of good health), and holiday packages (secret hideaways a specialty). If it engages the customer in even just a moment of consideration of the product – "What could it be?" or simply, "Why is it so hush-hush?" – secrecy helps to sell.

But what, you may well ask, is the secret of successful secrecy? Obviously, it's that the existence of a secret must never be kept secret. There's no point in having an exclusive product or service unless everyone who is anyone knows about it. But when big-budget marketing campaigns are unaffordable or inappropriate, what's a brand to do? The answer, and the third principle of retromarketing, is to *amplify* – that is, to ensure that the hot ticket or cool item is talked about and, more important, that the talking about is talked about.

The power of amplification can be seen in the recent buzz about "Ginger," the mysterious and much-talked-about creation by Dean Kamen. Widely regarded as the heir apparent to Thomas Edison, Kamen is a throwback to the amateur inventor archetype, a garage-based, gizmo-surrounded, patent-collecting tinkerer. He made his name – and his millions – with a portable insulin pump, a suitcase-sized dialysis machine, and, most recently, a gyroscopic, stair-climbing wheelchair. And now he has

## Time for a New Motown Revival

Of all industries, the automotive business is most responsible for perfecting the art of retro. It invented the Joe Isuzu–style salesman and has been quick to tap into nostalgic yearnings in its new model designs and advertising. How sad, then, to see the industry suppressing its true nature and embracing customer centricity as its marketing approach.

Just consider its retro credentials. The Mazda Miata, an homage to 1950s roadsters, which comes complete with a carefully pitched tailpipe note, was the first retro auto rollout. Its triumph in the marketplace set the entire motor industry on the road to yesterville. Fast followers include the Chrysler PT Cruiser, a pastiche of the upright sedans of the 1940s; the Jaguar S-Type, an affectionate nod to the style of the immortal Mark II, beloved by British police officers and their criminal counterparts; and, best of all, the New Beetle, which melds the distinctive shape of the old Beetle with the latest automotive technology to produce a modern car with anachronistic styling. Not to be outdone, the retro auto prototype, Mazda's Miata, recently celebrated its decade-long heritage with a tenth anniversary special edition, thus making it a neo retro auto.

Yet despite the success of the retro products, the automobile industry hasn't fully embraced retromarketing. For every old-style publicity stunt, there are dozens of oleaginous allusions to market responsiveness, customer care, and our duty is to serve. Saturn says it all.

Auto marketers are unnecessarily ashamed of their Artful Dodger antecedents. They try to hide inveigling away, to disguise their deceitful DNA, only to suffer from the return of retromarketing repressed. It's time for the madness to end. The return of Joe Isuzu is a start, but the therapy must go deeper. It's time, carmakers, to get in touch with your inner huckster.

created Ginger, the code name for what is allegedly the greatest invention since the sliced bread cliché. The Net-propelled speculation surrounding the invention, known simply as "IT," has been overwhelming. Starved for actual information about the invention, the media has scrambled to report on the reports of the media. In the process, Ginger's become famous for being famous, as historian Daniel Boorstin famously put it – and marketed for being unmarketed. To date, no one knows what IT is exactly, and the seer's not saying. All we know for certain is that IT is so revolutionary that entire cities will be retrofitted to accommodate IT. Seal off those sidewalks. Rip up those autoroutes. Tear down those tollbooths. Ginger's coming down the turnpike, powered by a perpetual-motion motor that runs on hot air and hyperbole. Surprisingly, no one seems to have noticed the echoes in this craze of a classic P.T. Barnum marketing caper of 1860. Barnum's "it" turned out to be an encephalitic giantess from New Jersey; Kamen, it seems, simply plans to encephalize the New Jersey expressways. Clearly, they're being born at more than one a minute these days.

In a world of incessant commercial chatter, amplification is vitally necessary, and it can be induced in many ways beyond just mystery. One of the most cost-effective techniques is affront. Whether it be Calvin Klein, Benetton, or even Citroën – its Picasso minivan tweaked French aesthetes by appropriating the master's moniker – there's nothing like a little outrage to attract attention and turn a tiny advertising spend into a megabudget monster. Better yet, it bestows an aura of attractive insouciance on the I-fought-the-law offenders.

Another powerful amplifier is surprise. An unexpected marketing campaign can send shock waves through the media – as when Pizza Hut paid to have its logo placed on the side of a Russian rocket, or when Taco Bell offered a free taco to everyone in the United States if the decommissioned Mir managed to hit a 40-by-40-foot floating target placed at the anticipated splashdown site.

So much the better if all this marketing is *entertaining,* which brings us to principle number four of retromarketing: Marketing must divert. It must engage. It must amuse. Entertainment, in many ways, is the essence of retromarketing – and the lack of it is modern marketing's greatest failure.

I blame my esteemed colleague Philip Kotler, the renowned Northwestern University marketing professor, for this sorry state of affairs. He, more than anyone, has convinced managers that marketing is the backbone of business and must integrate the work of all other functions. Weighed down by this awesome responsibility, marketing has become a sober-sided discipline. It has lost its sense of fun. It has forgotten how to flirt.

The marketers of Hollywood, not surprisingly, have been resolute holdouts – not least in their latter-day use of the Internet. The Web site to promote the recent remake of *Planet of the Apes,* for example, contains an elaborate treasure hunt. *Swordfish's* site offers a $100,000 prize to anyone who can crack ten passwords. Most ambitious of all is the Web-based promotion of Steven Spielberg's *AI,* which premiered in June 2001. It's a surreptitious campaign, designed to be discovered and passed on from one cool person to another. Like the old record producer's trick of planting hidden messages between tracks (remember "I buried Paul"?), the process begins with a fake name inserted into the credits of a trailer for the movie. A Web search on that name leads the curious to a series of planted Web sites, a discovery of a murder, and a growing body of clues. Before long, cryptic e-mails and spooky phone messages come into play – and those who have followed the thread to that point are embroiled in a story quite separate from the film. Clearly, the marketers involved – highly aware that a movie lives or dies on its first two weeks of word of mouth – engineered a way to generate that buzz just before *AI* premiered. And it's more creative than concocting fake columnists or planting vox-pop puffery.

The *AI* campaign also exemplifies the final principle of retromarketing: marketing must deal in *tricksterism,* using tactics akin to those of Loki (of Norse myth), the wily Coyote (of Native American legend), and Hermes (the Greek god of the marketplace). The tricks don't have to be particularly elaborate; on the contrary, tricks can come cheap, as the now classic *Blair Witch Project* – is it a snuff movie or not? – bears eloquent witness. Similarly, the recent turn to sneaky sales promotions, where, for instance, the gregarious, round-buying barfly in the way-cool club is actually an employee of a liquor company, involves minimal expenditure on the marketer's part. However, the rewards can be great if the brand is embraced, even briefly, by the in-crowd.

There's nothing like a little outrage to attract attention and turn a tiny advertising spend into a megabudget monster.

A particularly sly bit of tricksterism was served up by the makers of Tango, a fruit juice soda popular in the United Kingdom. In 1994, the company bought advertising time and used it for what appeared to be a public service announcement; its "marketing director" warned viewers that some rogue supermarkets and convenience stores were selling a knockoff of the brand – it could be detected because it was not fizzy – and asked them to report the miscreant outlets by calling a special, toll-free hot line. Apparently, some 30,000 people rang up, only to be informed that they had been tricked ("Tango'd") as part of the company's promotion for a new, noncarbonated version of the drink. The ITC–Britain's TV-advertising watchdog–was not amused, and it rapped Tango's knuckles for abusing the public-information service format. In the meantime, the promotion had succeeded in amplifying the product launch and adding to Tango's incorrigibly irreverent image.

Being a trickster is not the same as being a downright cheater. Cheating, to state the obvious, is wrong, and people won't stand for it. The charlatanry I'm advocating comes with an extra dimension of panache, of exaggeration, of sheer chutzpah, which renders the unacceptable acceptable. Modern marketers set great store by the truth, and one can understand why, given marketing's less-than-illustrious heritage of diddling, double-dealing, and deceit. The truth, however, is that people don't want the truth, the whole truth, and nothing but the truth. And even if they did, the last place they'd look for it would be a marketing campaign. Marketing is about glitz and glamour. It's mischievous and mysterious. Marketing, lest we forget, is fun.

Marketing managers have fallen for their own line. They actually believe that if you love the customer enough, the customer will love you back. That is complete nonsense.

## From Four P's to Pure Tease

Retromarketing, then, is based on *exclusivity, secrecy, amplification, entertainment,* and *tricksterism.* At least this list of principles doesn't create an acronym...unless, of course, the sequence is reversed. To be sure, retromarketing is not appropriate on every occasion, nor is it applicable to every product, service, or market segment. But, then, the modern marketing concept of caring, sharing, all hold hands is not always the right approach, either.

Marketing managers, admittedly, may be dismayed by the thought of deliberately thwarting consumers. That's because they've fallen for their own line. They actually believe that if you love the customer enough, the customer will love you back. That is complete nonsense. Consumers, as a rule, don't love or care for marketing types, especially when they purport to have the customers' interests at heart. Consumers *want* to dislike marketers, they *like* to dislike marketers, they *need* someone to hate, particularly in politically correct times when ethnic stereotyping and other such nastiness is effectively forbidden. Contemporary consumers are embarrassed by marketers who get down on one knee and promise to love, honor, and obey. Get real! They would much prefer a good old-fashioned lovable rogue. Indeed, if marketers were *really* customer oriented, they'd give their customers what they want. Namely, old-style, gratuitously provocative marketing rather than the neutered, defanged, Disneyfied version that's peddled today.

Retromarketing, in sum, harks back to the good old bad old days when marketers were pranksters and proud of it. It replaces the Seven S's with seven veils. Its Five Forces are flim, flam, flirt, fiddle, and finagle. Its Four P's are perturb, puzzle, perplex, and perhaps. Its Three C's are chafe, chide, and chortle. It puts the mark into marketing, the con into concept, the cuss into customers. It's a marketing philosophy for a retro-besotted world. It's tried and true. It's the greatest show on earth.

Would I lie to you?

Reprint R0109E
To place an order, call 1-800-988-0886.

## UNCOVERING PATTERNS IN CYBERSHOPPING

(W. Moe and P. Fader / CMR210 / 12p)

### Summary

E-commerce managers, overwhelmed with customer data, have been focusing on aggregate-level summary statistics. Using commonly available clickstream data, the authors discuss the benefits of separating an individual customer's buying behavior into simple patterns of visits and purchasing conversion. This analysis of the buying process informs a more careful examination of the relationship between store visits and purchasing behavior.

### Outline

Separating Purchasing Behaviors
Understanding Visitor Traffic at Your Site
Conversion Behavior
Detecting Shopping Strategies
Discussion

### Learning Objective

Understand how to better leverage customer data on store visits and purchasing.

### Questions, Ideas, and Exercises

1. Before considering the application of the authors' ideas to your firm's Web site, pay close attention to your own behavior when browsing or buying online. Consider the "footprints" you leave behind in clickstream data. How long are you likely to examine various products in various circumstances? How strong is the relationship between "visiting behavior" and "purchase conversion"?

2. To what extent can marketers, salespeople, and product developers in your company obtain the clickstream-derived information that would be most useful in understanding consumer behavior? Is your Web team truly at your service in this respect, or are they attending to another agenda? Conversely, do you proactively seek to get the Web team's help in examining and understanding clickstream data?

CMR210
07/01/2001

# Uncovering Patterns in Cybershopping

Wendy W. Moe
Peter S. Fader

*California Management Review* Reprint Series

# Uncovering Patterns in Cybershopping

**Wendy W. Moe**
**Peter S. Fader**

Academics and practitioners alike have been arguing about whether the Internet brings a revolutionary change in the fundamental way we do business or if it simply offers a new distribution channel and communication medium. Regardless of the answer to that debate, one thing is for sure: the Internet provides managers with an enormous amount of customer information that was previously unavailable. Thus, the new struggle has been to manage this information and to accurately and efficiently use it to somehow measure customers, trends, and performance.

Of particular interest is the role of Internet clickstream data in customer relationship management by providing a rich source of behavioral information. Until recently, the bricks-and-mortar marketers have focused their measurement and modeling efforts primarily on easily available purchasing data. Marketing research vendors in various industries (e.g., Information Resources, Inc., for customer packaged goods; SoundScan for the music industry; and IMS for pharmaceuticals) have been able to provide manufacturers and retailers with rich information regarding market share, brand switching, and new product performance. However, the spotlight has generally been centered on ultimate purchasing activity—when, what, and how much people buy. Customer activities such as comparison shopping and information gathering have largely been ignored for lack of data. These behaviors may be less visible but still exert strong influences on purchasing. As managers attempt to alter customer behavior using marketing tactics such as advertising and web site design, it is critical to reach and persuade customers at these earlier stages of the decision process.

In contrast, e-commerce managers are often faced with the opportunity of having more data than they know what to do with—from their own transaction servers, customer log files, and a wide array of other new types of primary and secondary data sources. These "data warehouses" offer unique information on customer shopping behavior beyond just purchasing. However, there can be substantial costs to acquiring and managing this additional data; for a variety of reasons, many companies are unwilling or unable to proceed aggressively in this direction and therefore discard or ignore much of their available data.

Additionally, there has been a drastic decline in the e-commerce climate from the "irrational exuberance" experienced in the late 1990s. The current and more pessimistic view has led managers to severely cut "unnecessary" costs. The target of much of this cost cutting has been marketing—specifically, customer analysis, acquisition, and retention costs. However, in such environments, it is more important than ever to understand customers and focus on their needs in an effort to build stronger relationships that will endure. To this end, e-commerce managers should utilize their customer data to develop more efficient marketing strategies.

Hidden in the clickstream data available to many e-commerce sites is precious information that can provide better diagnostics and more accurate forecasts, allowing e-commerce sites to more profitably target and market to their customers. The key lies in the ability to better understand the data using the correct measures and models. The aim is to make the process as simple as possible, while fully acknowledging the complexities (and inherent randomness) that characterize shopping and purchasing behaviors.

There is a sharp distinction between this approach and so-called "data-mining" procedures. In data-mining methods, analysts merely "feed" the computer with dozens, perhaps hundreds, of different variables about buyers and their situational characteristics. The computer looks for patterns in the raw data with little regard for the validity (or lack) of any behavioral "stories" that might explain the associations they uncover.

In our approach, we first try to tell some appropriate stories starting at the level of the individual customer and then explicitly allow for differences across customers. Only after we have built up to an aggregate model in this fashion do we bring in the data to flesh out (and test) the behavioral assumptions we have made. If our "story" is not borne out well by the actual data, we reconsider certain assumptions and begin the process again. Our experiences in applying these methods to online visiting and purchasing patterns have been quite successful to date. This article reviews some of the patterns and methods that have emerged as dominant themes in our recent work.

## Separating Purchasing Behaviors

The shopping process consists of two separate behaviors. First, the customer must decide to visit the store, be it to gather information, evaluate options, or to look for something specific. Once in the store, the same customer must decide whether or not to buy during that store visit. Customer online

**FIGURE 1.** Purchasing Process

behavior can be seen as a process starting with the decision to visit a store and ideally ending with a purchase (Figure 1). Consequently, fully understanding purchasing behavior entails the analysis of several intermediate steps and is more complicated than analyzing just the purchasing events.

Over time, a customer's behavior at a store can be characterized by a pattern of visits and a pattern of purchases. However, since not all visits end in a purchase, understanding purchasing patterns is not at all equivalent to understanding visit patterns. Instead, two separate behaviors underlie purchasing: visiting and "conversion" from being a mere browser to an actual buyer. Therefore, two different models are needed to accurately capture the customer's shopping process. It is very useful and instructive to view these modeling exercises as being separate. Each sub-model has a unique set of behavioral and statistical issues associated with it and, in turn, each one provides a unique set of managerial diagnostics that can be used to properly gauge the effectiveness of marketing actions.

Consider the struggles that e-commerce managers have had in attempting to sort through the many metrics available to them in an effort to find the single best yardstick on which to focus. Even after the enormous shakeout that began in the spring of 2000, many sites still stress visitor traffic as the primary indicator of success. Accordingly, many sites have dedicated considerable resources to increase visitor traffic, either by attracting new users with mass media advertising campaigns or by cultivating repeat visitor traffic with e-mail campaigns.

However, with many popular sites still not turning a profit despite their high visitor traffic, other managers have begun to value the conversion rate metric (percent of visits that end in a purchase). Sites that evaluate their success based on their conversion rate tend to invest in "in-store" promotions and price discounts to induce the visitor to buy. If e-commerce managers need to allocate their marketing resources between these strategies, they must be able to accurately evaluate their visitor traffic and purchase conversion rates rather than just having a vague notion of overall site performance. Treating store visiting and purchase conversion as fundamentally separate behaviors more accurately forecasts overall purchasing than when the behaviors are combined within a single, more complex, model.

Merely separating purchasing into visits and conversion is not enough to provide the most accurate forecasts. Each model needs to consider the dynamics

**TABLE 1.** Summary of Visit Data over Time

| | Bookstore | | CD Store | |
|---|---|---|---|---|
| | Months 1-4 | Months 5-8 | Months 1-4 | Months 5-8 |
| Total Number of Visits | 5402 | 5899 | 1729 | 1890 |
| Number of Unique Visitors | 2693 | 2717 | 988 | 920 |
| Visits/Visitor | 2.01 | 2.17 | 1.75 | 2.05 |

that take place as customers gain experience with a particular site. Their visits may tend to speed up or slow down, and their conversion rates will likely be changing over time as well. As a result, their behaviors, in terms of store visiting rates and purchase conversion, are systematically shifting over time. Combining this evolutionary behavior in a model that separates the two aspects of purchasing more effectively describes and forecasts customer behavior.

## Understanding Visitor Traffic at Your Site[1]

As illustrated in Figure 1, the first component behavior driving ultimate purchasing patterns is store visiting. One of the first steps in building a retail store, both online and offline, is to bring people to the store. Therefore, it is very important for e-commerce managers to be able to accurately measure, monitor, and forecast visitor traffic at their site. Many available metrics refer to the number of visits and visitors to a given site in a specified period of time. To monitor changes, both improvements and declines, these numbers can be compared from one period to another.

As an illustration, imagine that overall visitor traffic has been increasing from one quarter to the next, as seen in Table 1. These figures suggest that not only are the numbers of unique visitors to the site increasing, but they are also visiting the store more frequently, as indicated by the increasing visits per visitor rates. This measure suggest that over time, shoppers begin adapting to the site and visit more frequently, thereby creating more buying opportunities—a very positive development for the site. However, this is a deceptively optimistic view of visitor traffic at the site.

One problem with examining aggregate numbers of visits and visitors, such as those presented in Table 1, is the issue of a changing customer base. In the case of e-commerce, as well as other new and developing markets, new customers are constantly entering—customers who may be fundamentally different in their rates of visit than those more experienced individuals (who may be exiting the market). As a result, such aggregate summary measure could simply be reflecting the inflow of new customers and the resulting change in customer base rather than any behavior evolution among the existing customer base.

**FIGURE 2.** Model Forecasting Plot

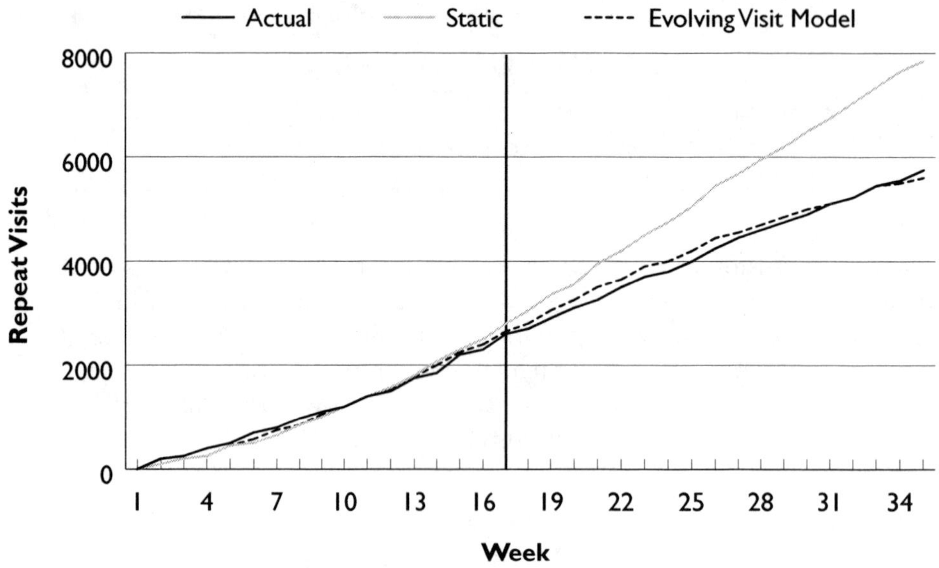


So, how should visitor traffic trends be modeled if these metrics are misleading and biased? Our approach employs very flexible but simple probability mixture models to allow for consumer heterogeneity as well as individual behavioral evolution. That is, we can model each individual shopper as having an inherent rate of visiting a site. This rate, from which we can derive inter-visit times, varies across individuals to accommodate differences within the population. However, as consumers visit a site repeatedly, their behavior may systematically change as a result, i.e., there may be *behavioral evolution* in visiting. Therefore, to accurately monitor changes in visiting behavior, we model each consumer's rate of visit for each visit as the rate governing the timing of the previous visit multiplied by a probabilistic updating multiplier ($\text{RATE}^{t} = \text{RATE}^{(t-1)} \times \text{UPDATE}^{t}$). The distribution of this updating multiplier provides a description of the trend in visit frequencies. For the same e-commerce site used in the examples above, an individual-level probability model reveals that visits are actually declining in frequency—contrary to the implications offered by the aggregate summary metrics offered in the above table.

Figure 2 offers a plot comparing the forecasts derived from a static model of visiting (i.e., not allowing for behavioral changes) versus one that does allows for behavioral evolution (including attrition). When behavior evolution is not accounted for, the model significantly over-estimates future visitor traffic as it does not allow individuals to change their behavior. Instead, it incorrectly assumes that historical behavior is an appropriate indicator of future behavior. The evolving visit model, which does accommodate behavioral evolution, is capable of providing extremely accurate forecasts of visitor traffic.

In addition to being able to discern trends in visiting behavior, characterizing individuals' visiting behavior in terms of just frequency and trends offers strong *indications of purchasing*. In general, those shoppers who make more frequent store visits are more likely to purchase in any given visit—this is true both online and offline. However, evolution in visiting frequency also provides a strong indicator of a shopper's purchasing propensity. Those who are visiting a store at an increasingly frequent rate also have higher conversion rates than those who are showing a slow down in their visit frequencies. Furthermore, those shoppers who are considered frequent visitors *and* are increasing their rates of visit reflect an interaction effect between frequency and evolution and are particularly attractive, in terms of conversion rates, to the e-commerce site (see Table 2 for an example).

**TABLE 2.** Visiting Patterns as Indicators of Purchasing Conversion Rates (CR)

| | **Decreasing Frequency** | **Increasing Frequency** |
|---|---|---|
| **Bookstore** | | |
| Infrequent Visitors | CR = 10.9% | CR = 11.3% |
| Frequent Visitors | CR = 14.6% | CR = 18.6% |
| **CD Store** | | |
| Infrequent Visitors | CR = 3.8% | CR = 5.7% |
| Frequent Visitors | CR = 4.0% | CR = 7.6% |

The differentiation between a shopper's visiting behavior and purchase conversion highlights the distinct roles of various marketing tools. Mass advertisements, targeted promotions, and brand-building efforts affect different stages in the consumer decision process. As such, they should be used differentially depending on the state of the site and the objectives of the e-commerce manager. For example, mass advertisements many generate awareness and drive traffic to the site. However, it does not necessarily have any impact on purchasing conversion. If the site's objective is indeed only to build traffic, the evolving visits model described above provides an effective method to evaluate the results of such a campaign. However, beyond just bringing in visitors, e-commerce sites must also consider the shopper's conversion decision once in the store. Likewise, tools designed to increase purchasing conversion and improve customer retention are quite distinct from tools designed to generate visitor traffic and may not have any effect on building traffic. The attention of marketing efforts at this stage of the game must shift from building awareness to building preference, purchase intentions, and—later on—customer retention. Hence, the marketing tactics available include building the brand, promoting to induce trial, and developing customer loyalty programs.

## Conversion Behavior[2]

Before deciding which purchase conversion campaign to pursue, we must first fully understand the shoppers' conversion behavior at the site. The Internet has made store visits very "cheap" for shoppers. As it is virtually costless for consumers to visit online stores, consumers are not as committed to buy when in an online store as when they travel to visit a bricks-and-mortar store. This makes store traffic management a more important issue online than offline. Though high store traffic provides more buying opportunities, there is a tradeoff—heavy traffic is also expensive for e-commerce sites to accommodate. Therefore, it is important in any cost reduction efforts for an e-commerce site to differentiate between their shoppers and prioritize them for targeting purposes.

As noted, one way to differentiate visitors is by their visit frequency and stage of evolution. However, another very appealing and more direct method of differentiating between visitors is by their likelihood of buying, or conversion probability. High-probability buyers should be identified, and e-commerce managers need to ensure that their experience at the site is positive—for example, by channeling them to a faster server or offering service "perks." Low-probability buyers should also be identified as potential targets for promotions. Though these shoppers are not necessarily more promotion sensitive, it is more cost efficient to promote to unlikely buyers and persuade them to buy than it is to promote to shoppers who are likely to buy without any added incentive.

The challenge is to assess each visitor's likelihood of buying as they enter the site. Sales personnel perform this task at bricks-and-mortar stores, to varying success. In the virtual environment, one available measure it to examine each individual's historical conversion rate (the number of purchases made divided by the number of visits) and assume that this rate governs purchasing probabilities for all future store visits. However, there are several weaknesses to this approach. First, many visitors have very limited histories, i.e., they are relatively new visitors to the store. Without any information on that individual's visiting and purchasing history, there can be little faith in the ability of historical rates to predict future purchasing probabilities. For example, someone who has visited only once in the past and purchased during that visit is unlikely to exhibit a 100% conversion rate in the future. It is more likely that the purchase made was a chance result of a much lower conversion probability. Second, an individual's purchasing probabilities are not necessarily unchanging from visit to visit. A shopper may have buying cycles, e.g., they may visit an online store fairly regularly but may only purchase every other visit. In this case, their probability of buying changes fairly systematically from one visit to the next. In addition to cyclical changes in buying probabilities, there may also be fundamental changes that result from the shopper evolving with every visit and/or purchase. For example, as shoppers gain experience from repeated purchases, does this fundamentally change their latent propensity to buy in future visits?

Again, to solve this problem, we turn to individual-level probability models. In this case, we can model each customer as having an inherent conversion rate (or probability of buying at any given visit). Again, each individual's conversion probability is different and must be modeled as a heterogeneous trait. Furthermore, an individual's conversion probability is affected by his/her history of visits and purchases. The result is a model of conversion behavior that allows a shopper's conversion probability to change from visit to visit, be it as a result of evolution or a systematic purchasing cycle.

There are two sources of such *non-stationarity* (or changes in conversion probability): *cyclical changes* and *behavioral evolution*. First, cyclical changes may result from shoppers making a number of visits before each purchase, perhaps for the purpose of accumulating information prior to the purchase. In these cases, there is a systematic purchasing cycle in terms of visits, i.e., the shopper buys something once every *x* visits. Second, purchasing may also be cyclical in terms of calendar time. For example, some shoppers may visit the store irrespective of whether they intend to buy. Instead, purchases are made regularly every *x* days. In these illustrations, conversion probabilities may systematically change as the shopper makes repeat visits or as time passes.

In addition to the cyclical changes in purchase conversion, there may also be evolution in buying tendencies brought on by repeat visits and/or purchases causing more permanent changes. For example, as a shopper visits a site repeatedly, he or she may become accustomed to the site, and the effectiveness of each store visit in inducing a purchase may increase or decrease. Additionally, purchases may also fundamentally change a shopper's conversion behavior. That is, as individuals make repeated purchases, they may change their attitudes toward purchasing from the site. Many shoppers are reluctant to buy from an unfamiliar store site the first time, but as they gain purchasing experience, they become more comfortable with the site and may be more likely to buy. Curiously, research has shown that repeated purchases tend to decrease a customer's tendencies to buy from that site in the future, suggesting that there is an initial novelty effect that slowly wears away.

Therefore, when examining conversion rates, the e-commerce manager must realize that purchasing conversion is more complicated than just a single summary measure of purchases to visits. Instead, individuals have very different purchasing tendencies from one another. The ability to differentiate individual visitors by their purchasing probabilities provide e-commerce managers with more valuable information regarding each shopper's value as a customer as well as how to best serve them. Additionally, one must recognize that purchasing probabilities not only vary across individuals, but also change within individuals from visit to visit. Understanding how these probabilities change from visit to visit, as a result of visiting and/or purchasing experiences, provides information useful in forming marketing strategy. For example, are shoppers slow to convert? If this is the site's source of weakness, marketing resources should focus

**TABLE 3.** Taxonomy of Shopping Strategies

| Timing | Motivation | |
|---|---|---|
| | **Planned Purchase** | **No Planned Purchase** |
| Immediate Purchase | Directed-Purchase Visit | Hedonic Browsing Visit |
| Future Purchase | Search/Deliberation Visit | Knowledge-Building Visit |

on inducing trial and converting the non-buyers (or not-yet-buyers). On the other hand, if customer attrition is the source of problems, the site would be better served not by inducing trial or even building traffic, but by investing in customer retention and loyalty.

## Detecting Shopping Strategies[3]

A unique aspect of Internet clickstream data is its ability to provide information on a variety of different consumer shopping strategies. For example, some consumers are going to the store with a very specific purchase in mind. In those cases, their store visit is very directed and will almost certainly end in a purchase. In other cases, the shopper is interested purely in browsing, and the visit may or may not end in a purchase, depending on what the individual encounters during the visit. The question is, are there store visit characteristics, that can be found in navigational clickstream data, indicating the predominant shopping strategy?

Table 3 offers a taxonomy of different shopping strategies that vary along two dimensions: the *motivation* behind the shopping trip and the *timing* of any resulting purchase. Motivation refers to the underlying benefit (or utility) each store visit provides. Some store visits are made with a specific purchase in mind, and the decision to visit the store is simply a means to that end (*planned purchase*). Other visits, however, are not made for the purpose of a purchasing decision. Instead, the shopper derives pleasure from the simple act of visiting and exploring the store (*no planned purchase*). Both motivations can result in a purchase, either immediately or some time in the future.

The framework offered in Table 3 characterizes store visits by these different motivations and purchase timing into four shopping strategies: *directed-purchase* visits, *search/deliberation* visits, *hedonic browsing* visits, and *knowledge-building* visits. Directed purchase visits refer to those situations where the shopper enters the store with a clearly defined purpose of walking out with a specific purchase. Examples of this type of behavior are prevalent in grocery store visits. Search/ deliberation visits describe those visits where a future purchase is being considered, and the store visit is designed to gather relevant information needed to make a purchasing decision (e.g., pre-purchase visits to a car dealership). Hedonic browsing visits are store visits where the shopper enjoys the process and is not necessarily looking for anything specific. Instead, these visits are inherently valuable to the shopper as browsing experiences. However, an immediate purchase may still occur as an "impulse" depending on what the individual encounters during the visit (e.g., clothes shopping). Knowledge-building visits are also visits where the shopper enjoys the process itself. The difference lies in the timing of any potential purchase. Shoppers engage in knowledge-building visits to gather useful information regarding the market environment that may be used for a future purchasing decision (e.g., attending trade shows).

So, what differentiates each of these shopping strategies in clickstream data? Directed purchased visits tend to be very focused sessions. In other words, the shopper has a plan of attack and will not likely deviate from it. The resulting store visit is one that can be described as having limited variety in the number of different categories and products being viewed. Furthermore, as directed purchasers are close to making a purchasing decision, they are likely to deliberate on one specific product. This is often manifested by repeat product page viewings. Therefore, when e-commerce sites observe sessions where the shopper views few categories and repeatedly views a product page, one can speculate that the shopper is purchase-directed. In these cases, it is not cost effective to promote to these shoppers as they are fairly goal-directed in their behavior and are likely to buy without any added incentive of promotions.

Search/deliberation visitors are also fairly goal-driven. The difference is how close to buying the shopper is. Search/deliberation visitors are in the market for a specific type of product but are still seeking information to help make their decision. Therefore, these sessions tend to focus on a limited number of product categories but can involve viewing multiple products in the category. In other words, these sessions have a high product-to-category ratio. These sessions will also involve deeper drill-down of product information and longer viewing time per page to process the information. When visits are identified as search/deliberation visits, according to their product-to-category ratio and level of product drill-down, a *utilitarian* market message can better affect the shopper's purchasing decision. That is, since these shoppers are actively considering and evaluating product information, they may be more responsive to promotions that reduce price or highlight positive product attributes.

Hedonic browsing visits are very different from both purchase-directed and search/deliberation visits. Hedonic browsing sessions will tend to be much shallower in nature. That is, the time spent per page is short and product drill-down is minimal. Furthermore, as hedonic browsers are not shopping with any particular product in mind, they might view a number of different categories leading to a low product-to-category ratio. Most purchases resulting from these shopping sessions are impulse purchases stimulated by attention-grabbing attributes of the environment. Therefore, to best promote to these shoppers and increase their purchase conversion, e-commerce marketers should target the hedonic browsers with flashy and attractive promotions rather than with messages focused on objective product attributes.

Finally, knowledge-building visits are driven by the shopper's desire to learn about the product category and environment. As such, the session can be characterized by long page-viewing duration and a large percentage of the session spent on information related pages, such as advice columns, community areas, and company information pages. These shoppers are primarily interested in learning and not buying, at least not yet. Therefore, the e-commerce site is wise not to promote to them (at the risk of "spamming" their shoppers), as these shoppers are unlikely to respond.

The large numbers of customers entering an e-commerce site vary widely in their behavioral patterns and motivations. The ability to characterize a shopper's in-store behavior and infer the purpose of the store visit allows e-commerce marketers to better segment their customers and target them with the appropriate messages. In other words, a customer's experience at a site can be customized by analyzing the individual's observed navigational clickstream data. The e-commerce marketer can offer targeted promotions with messages customized for a specific type of shopper or provide enhanced customer service when appropriate.

## Discussion

If e-commerce managers wish to effectively allocate their marketing resources across activities, they must carefully consider the costs and benefits of pursuing each campaign. Whether the marketer is considering an advertising schedule to increase visitor traffic, targeted promotions to improve conversion rates, or loyalty programs to build customer retention, one must carefully separate purchasing into its component parts (as seen in Figure 1) in order to assess the potential effects of these marketing activities. For example, if an advertising campaign attracts a number of new visitors, how likely are they to purchase? For how long will they remain active customers? Models that carefully address the many aspects underlying customer purchasing can answer these questions.

Furthermore, the Internet is an ideal medium for e-commerce marketers to experiment with minor adjustments in their store environments and promotions in an effort to identify the most effective marketing mix. What is the ideal layout of the products? Which advertisements and promotions are the most effective and on which group of customers? Which items are more effectively cross-sold? The ease with which an e-commerce retailer can experiment with various attributes of their selling environment, coupled with the richness of data that the Internet is able to offer, provides marketers with an opportunity. With the right metrics and models, marketers can learn more about their customers and what they respond to better than ever before.

## Notes

1. Wendy W. Moe and Peter S. Fader, "Capturing Evolving Visit Behavior in Click-stream Data," Wharton Marketing Department Working Paper, 2000.
2. Wendy W. Moe and Peter S. Fader, "Which Visits Lead to Purchases?: Dynamic Conversion Behavior at E-Commerce Sites," Wharton Marketing Department Working Paper, 2000.
3. Wendy W. Moe, "Buying, Search, or Browsing: Using In-Store Navigational Click-stream to Identify a Typology of Store Visits," Working Paper, 2001.

significantly influence calculation of what is acceptable and what is not. Walkaways thus should take into account all of your various interests—tangible and otherwise.

By contrast, a rigid bottom line can be dangerous in two different ways. It can become a self-fulfilling prophecy, one that leads you to get a result close to your minimum. More important, a hard dollars-and-cents hurdle can blind you to creative solutions. For example, a bidder in the cable case might propose some sort of financing package at a generous interest rate. With favorable terms, the nominal price might turn out to be less important.

Sometimes you may be lucky and have an excellent BATNA. That would be true if you were negotiating with a prospective employer after already getting an outstanding offer from another firm. Then again, sometimes your BATNA can be terrible. If you were trying to get a hotel room on a busy holiday weekend, with your kids carsick from too much fast-food and your over-heated engine spewing radiator coolant, your walkaway would be grim. In that situation, you wouldn't demand that the desk clerk give you the corporate room rate (although that's not to say that you shouldn't ask.)

Assessing BATNAs and walkaways—your own and those of other parties—involves both science and art. The former lies in specifying the plausible alternative agreements and rating which, on balance, would be best. The tools of decision analysis and micro-economics are well suited to this task.[2] But art is involved, too, particularly in imagining creative alternatives and weighing their relative value. Research shows that most people are not very good at evaluating BATNAs. Common failings include over-optimism, particularly in lawsuits where both plaintiffs and defendants convince themselves that they are in the right and will win.

Only by considering the perceived BATNAs of both the potential buyer and seller can one see if agreement is really possible—and, if so, whether there is a lot of room to bargain or just a little. Take our first example, involving Frank Park's possible sale of his local cable television system to the national firm, C-Com. To keep things simple at the start, assume that the parties are interested only in a straight cash transaction. Specifically, assume that Park is prepared to accept the other existing offer ($10,000,000 from Gulf Cable) unless C-Com is willing to do better. In turn, C-Com has done financial analysis that justifies its paying up to $13,000,000. Any amount above that figure could be better invested in alternative acquisitions.

In familiar terms, there thus would be a bargaining range from $10,000,000 to $13,000,000. For reasons that are explained later, it is more useful to call this range a "zone of possible agreement" (or ZOPA). Any price between those two figures obviously leaves both parties better off than they would be if they fail to make a deal. On the other hand, there is no "correct" figure or equilibrium. If each party knew the other's walkaway price, social ritual might lead them to split the difference, though actually any number within the ZOPA would be preferable to no deal for both of them.

Even negotiation experts disagree about whether such situations are "zero-sum." In one sense, they are in that any added dollar that the seller gains is a corresponding loss to the buyer. As a result, single-issue negotiations (such as those over price) are often called "distributive" in that a unit of value is distributed to one party or the other, but it cannot go to both. On the other hand, it is important to remember that by coming to agreement, the parties do generate gain. In this instance, a surplus of $3,000,000 is created (the difference between the walkaway prices of the buyer and the seller). Whatever price they settle on leaves them both better off than accepting impasse.

In practice, of course, it is hard for negotiators to have an accurate picture of the ZOPA. Even if they have rigorously analyzed their own BATNA and calculated a present value equivalent, their

---

[2] See, for example, Hammond, Kenney, and Raiffa, *Smart Choices* (Boston: Harvard Business School Press, 1999).